Reduced Working Hours

JOHN D. OWEN

Reduced Working Hours

Cure for Unemployment
or Economic Burden?

The Johns Hopkins University Press

Baltimore and London

The Johns Hopkins University Press, 701 West 40th Street, Baltimore, Maryland 21211
The Johns Hopkins Press Ltd., London

The paper used in this publication meets the minimum requirements of American National
Standard for Information Sciences—Permanence of Paper for Printed Library Materials,
ANSI Z39.48-1984.

Library of Congress Cataloging-in-Publication Data

Owen, John D.
Reduced working hours: cure for unemployment or economic burden? John D. Owen
p. cm.   Bibliography: p.   Includes index.
ISBN 0-8018-3784-7 (alk. paper)
   1. Hours of labor—United States. 2. Hours of labor—Europe.
3. Work sharing—United States. 4. Work sharing—Europe.
5. Unemployment. 6. Manpower policy. I. Title.
HD5124.O94 1989   331.25'72'0973—dc19   88-30352

CONTENTS

PART I. Recent Changes in Work Time: The United States and Western Europe

PART II. Medium-Term Effects of Reduced Work Time

PART III. Long-Term Effects of Reduced Work Time

PART IV. Implications of the Reduced Work Time Issue

FIGURES

TABLES

ACKNOWLEDGMENTS

MANY PEOPLE were helpful to me in writing this book. The General Electric Foundation provided two generous research grants, which afforded the basic funding for the project. The encouragement of Nicholas Perna and Judith Shapiro at General Electric was especially welcome in the early stages of the project. The Institute of Gerontology at Wayne State University (William Brazill, director) provided travel grants that enabled me to make two trips to Europe to further my research. A number of people at the U.S. Bureau of Labor Statistics were extremely generous with their time and expertise, including Jerome Mark, Edwin Dean, Kent Kunze, James Markey, Art Neef, Joyanna Moy, Patricia Cap de Ville, and the participants in a seminar on reduced work time at the bureau in the summer of 1987.

In Europe, Robert Hart, then at the Science Center in Berlin, gave me important assistance in 1986. His then-unpublished manuscript on reduced work time, as well as his published writings, were most useful. He also drew my attention to the ongoing research of a number of European economists in this field. Gunther Schmid, Christoph Deutschmann, and others at the Berlin Science Center were also helpful, as were social scientists at the other research centers I visited.

At a later stage, Jacob Mincer of Columbia University, Steven Spurr and other members of the Economics Department at Wayne State University—as well as an anonymous referee—gave useful criticisms of a draft of this book.

Reduced Working Hours

INTRODUCTION

IT IS TIME to consider the implications of a reduction in work time for Americans. The past ten years have seen a furious debate in Europe over work time. European trade unions have asked for sharp reductions in work time in order to "share the work." In 1979, the European Trade Union Confederation called for a 10 percent additional reduction in work time, and other advocates have made even more militant demands. Considerable progress has been made toward achieving such goals in several European countries. In virtually all of them, the struggle for work sharing continues, often with government support.

This issue is only beginning to be discussed seriously in the United States. Understandably, it has been delayed by the long economic growth and low unemployment in the United States. Moreover, efforts that might have been made to reduce work time have instead recently been diverted to obtaining legislation (now in place in eleven states) that encourages more variation in workweeks over the business cycle. But when the next major increase in unemployment raises the work-sharing issue as a serious policy option, the European view will have some plausible arguments in its favor.

For many decades, the United States boasted the shortest work time in the industrial world, but now we have fallen behind. To some, this is a good argument for a reduction in hours. In addition, a persuasive, if superficial, argument can be made that reducing the work time of the employed reduces the number of the unemployed. In Europe, this argument has been used to defend major, permanent reductions in work time.

However, the European experience has led economists there to develop careful analyses of the employment-generating potential of hours reduction, and their conclusions have generally been quite negative. They have cast doubt on the idea that a significant reduction in unemployment could be obtained from such measures and have pointed to a number of negative side effects (on output, inflation, and the balance of payments) that result from work sharing. In the United States, this discussion has been developed mostly in technical articles and monographs, with the help of considerable mathematics. Moreover, the discussion has usually been illustrated with European rather than American institutions. As a result, it has not received much attention here. The present study attempts to fill that gap.

The book is divided into three parts. Part 1 sets out the basic facts about work time, presenting data on weekly hours and on vacations and holidays since 1945 in four countries: the United States and the three largest economies in Western Europe—the Federal Republic of Germany, France, and the United Kingdom. These data are compiled from a variety of sources. The analysis shows how the Europeans in this period were consistently more aggressive in demanding and obtaining shorter work time. Part 1 concludes with an attempt to understand the different paths followed by the United States and Europe since World War II.

Part 2 sets out in a systematic but nonmathematical form the basic arguments used in the current debate over work sharing and summarizes the principal empirical findings used in that debate. An explanation is offered of the negative assessment made by many European economists.

Part 3 considers the long-term consequences for the United States if a major, permanent reduction in work time does take place. This subject has received only a little attention in the work-sharing debate. (European economists have had to devote their attention to the development of a critique of the short- or medium-term employment effects of proposed work-sharing policies.) But it is a necessary task. The record—both here and in Europe—is that, when hours are reduced for several years, they remain permanently at the lower level. And a major, permanent reduction in work time would have profound effects on the economy and society.

Various techniques are used to predict these effects. Econometric results are reviewed, where relevant. Several scenarios in which hours might be reduced are constructed. The basic economic philosophy employed is that human labor is (and will be in the foreseeable future) a vital ingredient in the prosperity of our economy and society. Hence, a reduction in labor input will impose real sacrifices. Specific long-term effects of work time reduction on major economic variables, such as national output and the tax base for government programs, are analyzed in some detail. A discussion of effects on leisure time, recreation spending, and metropolitan area development is also included. These analyses make clear the quite significant costs, as well as the benefits, of reduced work time.

The brief part 4 contains a chapter on policy recommendations and a summary of the main points of the book.

PART I

Recent Changes in Work Time:
The United States and
Western Europe

CHAPTER ONE

The United States

WORK TIME in the United States fell sharply between 1850 and 1950. Estimates of working hours per week range up to seventy or more in the earlier period. Since then, the forty-hour workweek has become the standard schedule. In the years since World War II, however, progress toward further reduction has been much slower. The extent of the slowdown depends upon the measure of work time used. This is in part because in the past forty years there have been divergent movements in such measures as the workweeks of establishments (the hours that machinery is in use or the hours that a retail store is open to the public); the workweeks scheduled by establishments for employees; and the total hours of work put in each week by the average worker.

Data on annual vacations and holidays provide interesting additional information but do not change the overall picture of a slowdown in work time reduction.

The Work Time of Capital

The workweek of capital—the hours of operation of business establishments, including manufacturing plant, retail stores, mines, insurance agencies, and other service sector facilities—probably equaled that of labor in the earlier days of industrialization. But that is apparently no longer the case. In a detailed study of capital utilization, Murray Foss concluded that the workweek of establishments has actually increased over the past sixty years. Foss found an overall increase of 3.6 percent in weekly hours of utilization from 1929 to 1950 and an additional 5 percent increase from 1950 to 1976. The increase was especially large in manufacturing, where Foss estimated an increase of 12.5 percent in the earlier period and 10.8 percent in the later period. Changes among the other sectors were more diverse: for example, Foss found a rise in retail trade of 6.1 percent for the period as a whole but declines in construction, services and insurance, and real estate.[1]

Stable or increased hours of operation of capital stock in a period of declining hours for people was managed by the increased use of traditional shift work in industry[2] and by a combination of overlapping shifts and an increase in part-time employment in retail trade and other service sectors.

Work Time per Job

One does find some significant reductions since the 1940s in the work time of nonsupervisory employees in nonagricultural establishments (see Table 1.1). True, average work time in the traditional core (manufacturing, mining, contract construction, transportation, and public utilities) has shown little change. However, work time was reduced substantially in the service sector, broadly defined. The workweek in the wholesale and retail trade industries fell by about nine hours, from over forty to less than thirty-two. More moderate but still substantial declines are seen in the other service sector industries: financial, insurance and real estate, and other services. Moreover, since employment in the service sector grew relative to the industrial core, the drop in work time in the former also contributed to a decline in the overall average.

The gap that now exists between work time in the industrial core and that in the service sector appears to be largely due to differences in the use of part-time employees. Establishment data do not break employees down

TABLE 1.1. Weekly Working Hours, Nonsupervisory Private Nonagricultural Employees, United States, 1947–1986

Year	Average	Manu-factur-ing	Mining	Construc-tion	Trade	Finance, Insurance, and Real Estate	Other Services	Trans-porta-tion and Public Utilities
1947		40.4	40.8	38.2	40.5	37.9		
1950		40.5	37.9	37.4	40.5	37.7		
1955		40.7	40.7	37.1	39.4	37.6		
1960		39.7	40.4	36.7	38.6	37.2		
1965	38.8	41.2	42.3	37.4	37.7	37.2	35.9	41.3
1970	37.1	39.8	42.7	37.3	35.3	36.7	34.4	40.5
1975	36.1	39.5	41.9	36.4	33.9	36.5	33.5	39.7
1980	35.3	39.7	43.3	37.0	32.2	35.2	32.6	39.6
1983	35.0	40.1	42.5	37.1	32.0	36.2	32.7	39.0
1986	34.8	40.7	42.2	37.4	31.4	36.4	32.5	39.2

Source: U.S. Department of Labor, *Employment and Earnings,* various issues.

into part time and full time, but other data sources indicate that, when those working less than thirty-five hours a week are excluded, there is little or no difference between average hours in the two sectors.[3] Sex differences also help to explain the lower working hours in the service sector, since women, who are more likely than men to work part time, tend to work in this sector. For example, data on occupations indicate that males in sales occupations work eleven hours a week more than do women. In service occupations, the gap is six hours.[4]

Work Time per Worker

Establishment data may both underestimate the number of hours worked by the average employee and exaggerate the decline over time. One reason for this is that an individual may work at two jobs. Official data on moonlighting are available from the Bureau of Labor Statistics' monthly *Current Population Survey*. (The *CPS* is a survey of individual households, rather than of business establishments.) These data indicate a two-job rate of about 6 percent.[5] Moreover, many observers believe that this is an underestimate of moonlighting: there is a large underground economy—work that is illegal in itself, or that is not in compliance with labor or other legislation, or that is not reported as income to the Internal Revenue Service. A moonlighter who works in the underground economy is unlikely to report such activity to a census interviewer.[6]

There is a second reason—less obvious but probably more important—why establishment data are not a good measure of changes in work time. The demographic composition of the labor force has changed, and, since different groups work different numbers of hours, this has influenced the statistical average of work time. However, it is not so clear that the hours of the individuals or groups that compose the labor force have changed. The bulk of the labor force in 1950 were males who were not in school. In the intervening years, this proportion fell sharply, as the proportion of women and students increased. If one wants to measure the work time of any one of these groups—adult men, adult women, or students—data for the work force as a whole provide a poor guide. Employed adult males work about seven hours more a week than do employed females, and employed students work about fifteen fewer hours than does the average woman worker.[7] Hence the declining proportion of nonstudent males in the work force has tended to reduce the statistical average of work time, quite apart from any changes that may have occurred in the schedules of any of the groups that compose the labor force.

The *Current Population Survey* does provide demographic detail. Figure 1.1 presents data based on this survey for nonstudent males from 1948

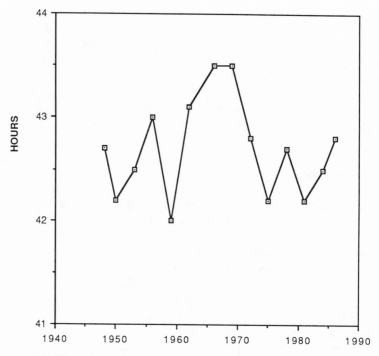

FIGURE 1.1. Weekly Hours, Nonstudent Males in Nonagricultural Wage and Salary Employment, 1948–1986

Sources: U.S. Department of Labor, *Employment and Earnings;* U.S. Department of Labor, *Special Reports on the Labor Force;* and Bureau of Labor Statistics, unpublished data.

to 1986.[8] This series shows no movement at all: weekly hours stood at 42.7 hours in 1948 and at 42.8 hours in 1986.

The distinction made here between the changes over time in the workweeks of the groups that make up the labor force and those in the arithmetic average is not simply a statistical quibble. The earlier, pre-World War II, reductions in the workweek represented very significant gains in the leisure time of American workers (then largely composed of nonstudent males). But the decline in the *average* workweek in the past forty years cannot be interpreted in this way. Insofar as the reduction represented a change in the composition of the work force, no further gain in leisure time had resulted. This abstract interpretation gains in plausibility when one considers that many members of the new groups in the work force—women and students—do a considerable amount of work outside of their market employment, housework and study. Their movement into the labor force, even at schedules of less than forty hours per week, presumably meant a *reduction* in their leisure.

A final judgment on leisure changes requires an analysis that goes far beyond the discussion of workweeks as such and so is beyond the scope of this study. Good arguments can be advanced for both views: that the leisure of the "average" American has increased and that it has decreased over the past forty or so years.[9] Work time data are of only limited value in determining the truth of the matter. The index that comes closest to a measure of leisure is the series on working hours of nonstudent males presented here, since this group has a minimum of outside or nonmarket work time responsibilities. At least, changes in it may reflect changes in the leisure of adult males during the workweek.[10] However, these data are also subject to criticism. They are based on a household survey, and though this survey is widely used (partly because of the demographic detail that it provides), it is generally regarded as somewhat less accurate than the data collected from establishments. Respondents to the household survey may be members of the family other than the earner, and these members may have an inaccurate notion of the earner's hours. It has been suggested that their estimates will be upward biased as well as inaccurate, since they will tend to underestimate lunch hours, to round up to forty hours a week, and to make other similar errors. (It could also be argued that the *Current Population Survey* underestimates moonlighting activity because interviewees are reluctant to discuss work in the underground economy with government representatives, so that the series will be biased downward.)

This leaves us in the uncomfortable position of having to choose between two data sources—the establishment and the household series—neither of which is perfect.[11] A compromise is possible, however. The establishment series is probably the better indicator of changes in the statistical average of workweeks over time, and this series does show some moderate downward movement since the end of World War II. But that movement overestimates the decline in the hours of adult males (or of the other groups that make up the labor force), since this period saw a major increase in the participation both of students and of women, and these both have much shorter work schedules. It also saw a significant amount of moonlighting. Hence, a more accurate appraisal would be that the work time of adult males has perhaps fallen somewhat, but by less than even the modest amount indicated by the establishment series.

Vacations and Holidays

The discussion to this point has focused on the workweek as a measure of work time, but changes in vacations and holidays also affect the amount

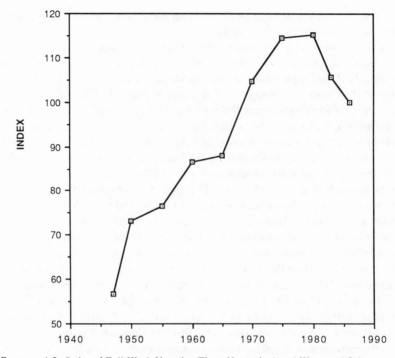

FIGURE 1.2. Index of Full-Week Vacation Time, Nonagricultural Wage and Salary Employees, 1948–1986 (1986 = 100)

Sources: U.S. Department of Labor, *Employment and Earnings;* U.S. Department of Labor, *Special Reports on the Labor Force.*

of leisure or work the employee has each year. It is often stated that growth in this time off has provided significant additions to the leisure of Americans, perhaps offsetting the much slower progress in workweek reduction in the years since World War II. However, available data provide only weak support for this view.

A *CPS* series on full weeks of vacation time per employee is available from the 1940s. It shows an increase of 77 percent over the past four decades (see figure 1.2).[12] This is an impressive growth. Yet it does not indicate that increases in vacations and holidays have been sufficient to offset the effects of the leveling off in weekly hours. No comparable historical data are available on annual holidays or on part-week vacations, but if one assumes that both grew at the same rate as full-week vacations, then the total of vacation and holiday time increased from about eleven days a year in 1947 to about twenty days a year in 1986.[13] When translated into hours per week (assuming an eight-hour day and a fifty-two-week year), one ob-

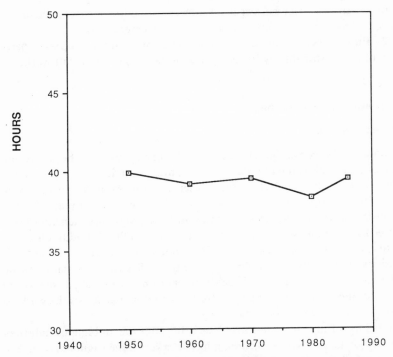

FIGURE 1.3. Hours of Work, Nonstudent Males in Nonagricultural Wage and Salary Employment, 1948–1986, Adjusted for Vacations and Holidays

Sources: Calculated from data in figures 1.1 and 1.2.

tains a workweek equivalent increase from 1.8 hours in 1947 to 3.3 hours in 1986. This 1.5-hour gain does not constitute a very impressive change. This can be seen in figure 1.3. Here, the data for weekly hours of work for nonstudent males charted in figure 1.1 are adjusted for vacations and holidays, using the data underlying figure 1.2.[14] Very little net change is observed here from 1960 to 1986.

Conclusions

1. The available data indicate that reductions in the work time of employed Americans from 1948 to 1986 have probably not declined as rapidly as in comparable earlier periods. Assessment is difficult because of gaps in the data, changes in the demographic mix of the labor force, and a tendency of workers to take time off in the form of more vacation and holidays

rather than as shorter workweeks. But even with adjustments for these factors, a slow rate of decline in work time is observed.

2. Employers have apparently been able to maintain the hours of operation of establishments by increased use of part-timers and shift workers.

Appendix to Chapter One

WORK BREAKS

Both of the conventional measures of working hours—the household survey and establishment data—can be faulted as indexes of work and leisure because they neglect on-the-job leisure. For example, in collecting data for a survey of hours at work at establishments, the Bureau of Labor Statistics instructs the employer to exclude holidays, vacations, and sick time from the measure of work time, but to include, "in addition to the actual time the worker is engaged in productive activities . . . short rest periods, coffee breaks, standby or ready time, downtime, portal-to-portal time (if paid), washup time (if paid), travel from job site to job site within the working day, travel time away from home if it cuts across the working day and paid training periods."[15]

This list of miscellaneous activities brings out the ambiguous nature of on-the-job leisure. Until recently, it has been very largely ignored by economists as a dimension of labor supply, but there is now a body of theory that discusses empirical estimates that measure on-the-job leisure. A recent study of time use carried out for households by the Institute for Social Research found that the average employed individual spends forty-five minutes a day in scheduled and unscheduled work breaks (apart from lunch times),[16] or 9 percent of all time spent at work by this sample. The authors of this study speculated that there has been an increase over time in break time and examined some fragmentary evidence that may support this view. Clearly, more empirical evidence would be welcome on this point.

It is even more important that we improve our analytical understanding of work breaks. It is not obvious that all this time should be treated as leisure rather than as work. The authors of the ISR study stated that "these breaks are partial measures of production sacrificed for other goals."[17] Where this is the case, the work break fits one definition of leisure widely used by economists. But break time often is *not* time taken at the expense of production. Break time can serve a productive purpose, or it may be simply unavoidable. In many job situations, time spent in breaks can be helpful in furthering productive relations among employees. For example, an economist working for a large corporation may find it useful to take coffee breaks with employees in other departments to help insure that accurate and full information will be forthcoming from these departments when needed by the economics division. Similar considerations govern the behavior of employees in many occupations, including blue collar jobs.

Work breaks may also be productive when they provide a needed respite. Indeed, a worker may find that he can maximize his daily output by working in spurts—that is, by taking periodic rest breaks, rather than endeavoring to work continuously.[18] In still other job situations, work breaks are forced on the employee by the conditions of production. Under these circumstances, break time is not at the expense of production. Indeed, enforced breaks can be quite boring and less pleasant than time spent on the task. Such interludes occur in the service sector during a falloff in the flow of customers. In manufacturing, they may occur when the machinery is down or because of the rhythms of the machinery itself.

This argument over work breaks is hardly new. Andrew Ure (sometimes called the poet of the factory system) was an early and enthusiastic supporter of the view that work breaks should be considered leisure. He was outraged by the inability of outsiders to understand the benefits that the early nineteenth-century English factory system brought to the children employed in the mills and argued vigorously against legislation calling for a reduction in the labor of children from twelve hours per day. In an 1832 essay written in opposition to this legislation, Ure noted that machines used in fine spinning "stand idle for . . . three-quarters of a minute, or more. . . . Consequently, if a child remains at this business twelve hours daily, he has nine hours of inaction. And though he attends two mules, he has still six hours of nonexertion. Spinners sometimes dedicate these intervals to the perusal of books."[19]

But despite the long history of argument for the work-breaks-as-leisure view, work breaks remain a controversial and difficult-to-analyze form of time use.

VACATIONS AND HOLIDAYS

There is, surprisingly, no good measure of vacation and holiday time actually taken in the United States. There are good data available on vacation and holiday provisions of union contracts. The U.S. Bureau of Labor Statistics also publishes data on vacations and holiday provisions for a national sample of medium- and large-sized firms. Both indicate rather generous provisions for high-seniority workers. For example, in the typical large or medium firm, the average employee obtains about four weeks of paid vacation after twenty years.[20] In some key sectors of the economy, union contracts provide even better benefits. But such data may be misleading. Many workers are employed in small firms, and these offer much inferior terms. Moreover, only a fifth of the work force is unionized. Finally, the generous provisions quoted above are available only to high-seniority workers. Even when small companies are excluded, one finds that the average firm gives less than nine days of vacation after one year of service and only two weeks after three years. But the average length a worker holds a job in the United States is about three years.[21]

Another difficulty is that vacation time provided is not the same as vacation time taken. In this survey, "sixteen percent of the plan participants were allowed to cash in unused vacation time."[22] On the other hand, some employees may take unpaid vacation time, which is not included in this survey. (This practice may be more common among small employers, who do not offer such generous paid vacation plans.)

Data on time taken as vacation or holiday is provided by the *Current Population Survey*. Each month, the survey asks about vacation and holiday time in the week preceding the survey, and an annual average of these estimates can be constructed from these data.[23] Unfortunately, this provides an imperfect measure, since the survey week is chosen so as to avoid major holidays. As a result, holiday time is grossly underestimated. Moreover, it has been shown that vacation time is also underestimated because workers often take their vacations in conjunction with major holidays. It has been estimated that this yields an underestimate of 20 percent.[24] Without this adjustment, the *CPS* data yielded an average of 9.5 days of vacation time in 1985 for all nonagricultural employees.[25] The 20 percent adjustment would raise this to 11.4 days.

But to obtain vacation and holiday time, one must also estimate the average number of holidays, and this is a most difficult task. The survey of medium and large firms indicate an average of 10.1 paid holidays per year. Ten days is probably too high an estimate of the required adjustment to the *CPS* data. The survey notes that "extended holiday plans, such as the Christmas–New Year's Day period provided in the auto industry, floating holidays, and 'personal holidays,' such as employee birthdays, were included in the holiday plans reported."[26]

Some of the extended holiday time included here may also be counted in the vacation time estimate of the *CPS*, and so should not be added here as an adjustment to it. More important, the exclusion of small firms very likely imposes an upward bias on this measure of holidays. Noting that 35 percent of these medium- and large-sized firms offer nine or fewer days off as holidays, a figure of nine days is employed here as a more reasonable estimate of the required adjustment. This yields an estimate of about twenty days per year of time taken in vacations and holidays.

This estimate can be confirmed by an alternative method of calculating vacation and holiday time. Here, one begins with the BLS hours-at-work survey of establishments, which does include small as well as medium and large firms and which collects data on both hours paid for and hours worked. In 1985, the survey indicated that time paid for but not worked was 6.5 percent of total time paid for.[27] The BLS states that this provides an estimate of the total of time for paid vacations, holidays, absence for illness and injury, and other paid absences.[28]

In a separate survey, the BLS collects data on time lost for absences for illness and injury and for miscellaneous reasons. These data can be used to obtain an estimate of paid time for these various employee absences: 1 percent.[29] This can then be subtracted from total time paid for but not worked, to obtain an estimate of 5.5 percent for paid vacation and holidays and for time off at the employer's discretion, as when a work site is closed due to bad weather. BLS data indicate that the last category accounts for a very small proportion of total hours (probably much less than 0.5 percent), and so no further adjustment is made for it here.[30]

The estimate of paid vacation time can be converted into an estimate of total vacation time by using a breakdown of total vacation time into paid and unpaid, provided by the *CPS* data on full-week vacations. These indicate that total full-week vacation time is 138 percent of paid full-week vacation time. No comparable data are offered for unpaid part-week vacations or for holidays, so the ratio for full-week vacation time is used here. This will again yield an overestimate if unpaid holidays are less common than unpaid vacation time. Following this method, an estimate of 7.6 percent of time for vacation and holidays is obtained: 19.8, or roughly 20 days for vacations and holidays per year. Thus this alternative estimate is almost identical to the original calculation.

This level of vacation and holiday time clearly represents a major improvement over conditions in the postwar period. However, it is difficult to obtain a quantitative measure of the improvement. Early data on vacations and holidays are extremely difficult to find. Much of the writing on holidays in the decades after the war analyzed an important shift: that unpaid time for blue collar workers became paid time off. As Peter Henle noted, "Before World War II, while major holidays were frequently observed throughout industry, the practice of providing pay for hourly rated employees was quite rare."[31] During the war, paid vacations and holidays were introduced for more blue collar workers, and in the postwar period the practice became quite common.

But while much is known about the growth of paid holidays, little is known about the extent to which this represents an increase in the actual number of holidays taken. Certainly, half a dozen or more major holidays were celebrated in many, if not most, establishments in the late 1940s. Hence, the increase in paid holidays would yield a misleading estimate of total holiday growth. As noted, a *CPS* series on full-week vacations is available from the 1940s, and this indicates an increase of 77 percent over the past four decades (see figure 1.2). This may provide an approximate measure of the upward trend in total vacation and holiday time in the postwar period.

DATA SOURCES FOR FIGURES

The weekly hours of nonstudent males charted in figure 1.1 were as follows: 1948, 42.7; 1950, 42.2; 1953, 42.5; 1956, 43.0; 1959, 42.0; 1962, 43.1; 1966, 43.5; 1969, 43.5; 1972, 42.8; 1975, 42.2; 1978, 42.7; 1981, 42.2; 1984, 42.5; and 1986, 42.8. The method of calculation is described in Owen, *Price of Leisure*. Essentially, data for all males in nonagricultural employment and data for male students in nonagricultural employment were used to derive a series for nonstudent males in nonagricultural employment. For example, in 1986 5.2 percent of males in nonagricultural employment were students, 94.8 percent nonstudents. Hours of work of all male employees in this sector averaged 41.9; of male students, 21.9. Using the formula 0.948 (hours of nonstudent males) + 0.052 (21.9) = 41.9 and solving for hours of nonstudent males yields 43.0 for that year. Adjusting for the 0.2 hours per week difference between all those employed in nonagricultural employment and wage and salary workers in that sector yields 42.8 hours. (Further details available on request from author.)

Figure 1.2, the index of full-week vacation time, was based on the following annual calculations: 1947, 56.6; 1950, 73.1; 1955, 76.4; 1960, 86.6; 1965, 87.9; 1970, 104.7; 1975, 114.6; 1980, 115.3; 1983, 105.7; and 1986 (the base year), 100. Estimates were obtained by taking the ratio of the number of nonagricultural wage and salary employees on vacation (annual basis) to total nonagricultural wage and salary employment. The 1986 ratio (2,973/98,251 = .0303) was then set equal to 100, and ratios in earlier years were expressed as a percentage of 1986.[32] The 1970 estimates were obtained from all nonagricultural employment data by interpolation of difference between this series and that for nonagricultural wage and salary employees. Estimates for 1947, 1950, and 1955 were obtained by adding a constant to the data for all employees equal to the difference in 1958 between this series and that for nonagricultural wage and salary employees.

The weekly hours of nonstudent males (adjusted for vacations and holidays) charted in figure 1.3 were as follows: 1950, 39.9; 1960, 39.2; 1970, 39.5; 1980, 38.3; and 1986, 39.5. To obtain the 1986 estimate, hours of nonstudent males (figure 1.1) were multiplied by .924 (see text).[33] The 1986 vacation and holiday adjustment factor was then extended back in time, using the index in figure 1.2.

CHAPTER TWO

Western Europe

THE REDUCTION of work time in the decades since World War II has proceeded more rapidly in Europe than in the United States. European work times are now usually shorter than in the United States, though they were significantly greater as recently as the 1940s. Table 2.1 gives percentage changes in hours of work in manufacturing in nine European countries, reflecting increases in annual vacations and holidays as well as reductions in the workweek. Substantial reductions—ranging from 14 to 29 percent—are observed in each country. Comparable data on annual hours in manufacturing in the United States are not available, but data on average weekly hours actually show an increase of 0.7 percent in this thirty-six-year period,[1] and, as was noted above, downward adjustment for increases in vacations and holidays in the United States would yield only a modest decline in the hours estimate.

In order to highlight some more specific differences between the United States and Western Europe, we will examine work time data for the three largest European economies, the Federal Republic of Germany, France, and the United Kingdom, then attempt to explain differences between their work time patterns and those of the United States.

Federal Republic of Germany

German workers have achieved impressive reductions in work time over the past forty years. The industrial workweek has declined sharply from the early 1950s: from forty-nine to forty-one hours for males and from forty-eight to forty-one hours for all workers, reflecting a reduction from a six-day, eight-hour-day workweek to a five-day, eight-hour-day workweek for most workers (see figure 2.1).

More detailed data available since 1960 (table 2.2) indicate that by that date the normal workweek (i.e., the agreed-upon, or standard workweek for full-time employees) stood at 5.5 days of 8.1-hour days.[2] By 1970, workdays were down to 5 a week, although daily hours were up to 8.3. No further reduction in standard workdays occurred in the 1970–85 period, but standard daily hours did decline to slightly less than 8 per day. Much

TABLE 2.1. Changes in Working Hours in
Manufacturing, Nine Western European Countries,
1950–1986, 1960–1986

	Percentage Drop in Hours Worked	
Country	1950–1986	1960–1986
Germany	28.6	20.8
France	16.8	16.8
United Kingdom	14.2	13.4
Netherlands[a]	24.3	25.2
Belgium[a]		22.4
Denmark	25.8	20.3
Sweden	28.9	24.3
Norway	20.9	17.9
Italy	19.5	22.3

Source: Calculated from U.S. Department of Labor, Bureau of
   Labor Statistics, June 1987 data.
[a]Change through 1985.

of the decline in the standard workweek had occurred by 1970: since that
time, it has fallen by only 5 percent.

Reductions below the forty-hour level have played an important role in
changes in the standard German workweek in the past several years. Forty-
three percent of German workers on full-time schedules now have a 38.5-
hour workweek, and 2 percent have hours less than that.[3]

The actual workweek has also been reduced by reductions in average
weekly overtime, from 3.63 hours in 1970 to 1.79 hours in 1985. Actual
hours have also been decreased by a sharp increase in part-time work.
Part-time work yielded a downward adjustment in this actual-hours series
of 4 percent in 1985, up from 1 percent two decades earlier. At the same
time, the actual workweek was increased slightly over this period by reductions in sick time and in shutdowns for bad weather. Interestingly, these
data indicate that changes in short-time working have had little effect on
the average workweek, despite government measures to encourage it.

In summary, after important reductions in the decades following World
War II, the standard West German workweek began to level off in the
mid-seventies. Important additional reductions continued in the actual
workweek though, largely because of reductions in overtime and increases
in short-time working (i.e., full-time employees temporarily on short-week

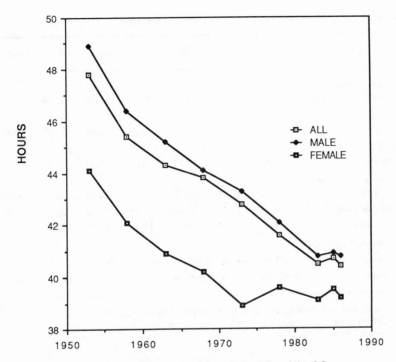

FIGURE 2.1. Weekly Working Hours in Industry, Federal Republic of Germany

Sources: *Statistiches Bundesamt,* October 1986; *Arbeits und Socialstatistik,* various issues.
Note: 1986 data through second quarter.

schedules) and especially because of increases in part-time work in the late seventies and early eighties.

The more recent slowdown in workweek reduction was offset in part by increases in vacation and holiday time. By 1960, there were over twenty-five vacation days and holidays per year, but the figure has since risen to forty-three days per year (about thirty days of scheduled vacation time and thirteen annual holidays). Such entitlements continued to grow rapidly in the seventies and eighties.

Even when this growth in vacations and holidays is taken into account, one observes some slowdown in the annual rate of decline in work time. Normal work time was reduced at the rate of 1.12 percent a year in the 1960–65 period, and at 0.65 percent a year in the 1980–85 period. (See table 2.2 for data on which these calculations are based.) When actual hours are examined, one obtains an annual rate of decline of 1.04 percent in the earlier period and 0.48 percent in the later period.

TABLE 2.2. Work Time, Federal Republic of Germany, 1960–1985

Item	1960	1965	1970	1975	1980	1985[a]	1986[b]
Weekly working hours	44.60	42.80	41.50	40.30	40.10	39.80	39.60
Weekly working days	5.50	5.25	5.00	5.00	5.00	5.00	5.00
Daily working hours	8.10	8.12	8.29	8.07	8.02	7.95	7.91
Yearly vacation days + holidays	25.32	27.90	32.10	36.48	39.63	42.90	42.70
vacation days	15.52	18.35	21.20	24.28	27.33	30.20	30.50
holidays	9.80	9.40	10.90	12.20	11.70	12.70	12.20
Yearly working hours normal	2,123.80	2,007.90	1,898.10	1,810.10	1,788.30	1,736.10	1,726.80
actual	2,080.80	1,975.80	1,888.00	1,736.50	1,688.30	1,641.60	1,628.70

Sources: *Statisches Bundesamt;* U.S. Department of Labor, June 1986.
[a]Preliminary data.
[b]Estimated data.

When these data on work time are compared with similar data for the United States, the major difference is of course that much better vacation and holiday benefits are enjoyed by German workers. Not only are better benefits afforded to high-seniority workers than is the case in the United States, but superior benefits are offered to beginning workers as well.[4] As a result of these benefits, the average German employee now has an annual schedule that is almost the equivalent of a four-day, eight-hour workweek. (Indeed, if the ten sick days per year are added to the forty-three vacation days and holidays, we get a total of fifty-three days per year, or approximately one day a week. Given a standard five-day workweek, this additional time off each year yields the equivalent of a four-day workweek.[5])

France

Considerable progress has also been made in reducing work time in France in the past forty years. Establishment and census data on weekly hours from 1945 to 1985 show a decline from forty-five hours in 1950 to less than forty hours in 1985 (see figures 2.2 and 2.3).[6]

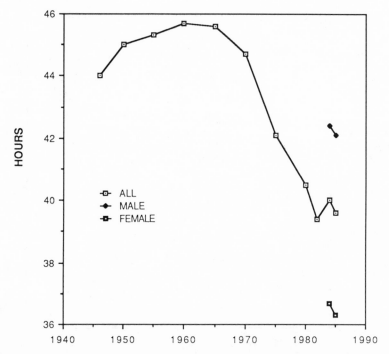

FIGURE 2.2. Weekly Hours Offered to French Employees (establishment data)

Sources: Samuel, *Le Temps libre,* p. 50; Marsden, *Working Time Statistics,* p. 117; INSEE, *Enquêtes sur l'emploi, 1984; 1985.*

These data are not adjusted for vacations and holidays, but French workers get five weeks of vacation per annum by law. (The history of legal minimum vacation allowances is given in table 2.3.) Many employers give more than the minimum, either to all employees or to high-seniority workers only. In addition, annual holidays and "bridges" (i.e., days linking holidays to weekends) account for an average of nine to ten days a year.

A 1985 study by the French institute INSEE endeavored to assess the impact of reductions in weekly hours and of increases in vacations and holidays on annual work time for the 1970–83 period. It found that the annual work time of nonagricultural employees fell between 1970 and 1983 by about 300 hours. The drop averaged about 20 hours a year between 1970 and 1981; then hours were reduced by 80 hours in 1982 (the combined result of a 1-hour reduction in the official workweek, from 40 to 39, and a one-week extension of the vacation period, from four to five weeks).[7] More recent estimates indicate that the rate of decline in work time in France has again slowed down. These data show a decline in annual hours

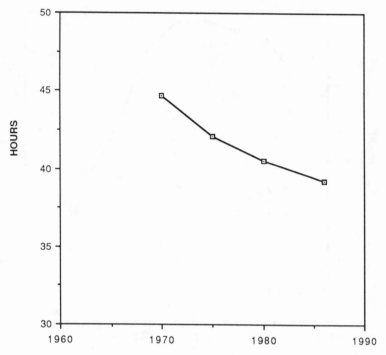

FIGURE 2.3. Weekly Hours Worked by French Employees (household survey data)

Sources: U.S. Department of Labor, *Working Time Statistics,* p. 116; Bureau of Labor Statistics, unpublished data.

from 1982 to 1986 of 42, or an annual rate of decline of 10.5 hours—much less than the annual decline observed in the decade before the 1982 legislation.[8]

The reduction in work time in France thus follows a pattern broadly similar to that observed in Germany (and indeed in the other countries of northwestern Europe). The French experience has been different in the timing of the change. The Popular Front government of Léon Blum enacted legislation in 1936 that called for the establishment of a forty-hour workweek, a standard well in advance of that in other nations. In practice, the forty-hour goal was not achieved, since many exceptions were allowed, but the influence of this legislation is said to explain why the French began the postwar period with a shorter workweek (about forty-five hours per week) than did some neighboring countries. This level of work time was maintained in France until the early seventies, while neighboring countries were making considerable progress toward achieving a forty-hour workweek. More recently, some significant reduction in working hours has taken place in France: weekly working hours fell below forty hours in 1986, while vacation days and holidays continued to increase. For the postwar period as a whole, a quite substantial decline in work time has therefore occurred in France.

The United Kingdom

Less detailed data are available for the United Kingdom, but the figures we do have indicate strong similarities with other European countries. Paul Blyton points out that "changes in weekly hours in Britain during the present century have been concentrated into four short periods: 1919–1920, 1946–49, 1960-2/64–6 and 1979–82. In general these periods saw the introduction of the 48, 44, 40 and 39 hour normal working week."[9]

The normal workweek continues to decline. A recent analysis of manual workers by the British government found that "fewer than 15 per cent still have basic weekly hours of 40 or more. A significant minority of employees (about 10 per cent of those covered in this analysis) now have basic hours of less than 39."[10]

It is important to bear in mind that these data pertain to "normal" hours, which exclude overtime. Overtime hours have traditionally been quite high for British workers: the average for all British males in manual occupations (including those with zero overtime) ranged from 4.7 to 6.3 hours per week in the 1975–84 period. On the other hand, short-time schedules are also worked. Hence movements in normal hours are a good guide neither to changes in actual hours, at least in the short or medium term, nor to the level of hours at a given time. In 1984, the normal weekly working hours of men and women in manual work were, respectively, 39.2 and 38.1; in nonmanual work, the normal hours of men and women averaged 37.1 and 36.1 per week. The series on actual hours indicate significantly higher levels, especially for male manual workers (see table 2.4).

TABLE 2.3. Legal Minimum Vacation Time, France

Year	Vacation Time
1936	12 days (2 weeks)
1956	18 days (3 weeks)
1969	24 days (4 weeks)
1982	30 days (5 weeks)

Note: A six-day workweek is assumed.

TABLE 2.4. Weekly Working Hours, British Manual
Workers, 1969–1986

Year	All Manual Workers	Male	Female
1969		46.5	38.1
1974		45.1	37.4
1979		44.0	37.4
1984	42.5	43.4	38.2
1985	42.8		
1986	42.7		

Source: *Employment Gazette,* various issues.
Note: Data are actual hours of full-time employees working at adult
rates; they exclude those whose pay was affected by absences.

However, actual hours of work for male manual workers on full-time
schedules also show a pattern of long-term decline, from 46.5 in 1969 to
43.4 hours in 1984. This indicates that any increase in overtime working
that might have occurred in this period was not sufficient to offset the decline in normal hours cited by Blyton.

Further, the omission of part-time jobs from these data also underestimates another source of decline in British hours. In discussing the rapid
growth of part-time employment in the United Kingdom, Olive Robinson
points out that, while the number of full-time employees has fallen by 2.3
million, there has been a rise of 3.7 million in part-timers. She adds that
"the latest employment estimates indicate that these trends are continuing."[11] This part-time employment is 84 percent female and almost 90 percent in services. (Part-timers here are defined as regular, voluntary part-
timers, working less than thirty hours a week.) This growth of part-time
employment suggests that the data in table 2.4 significantly underestimate
the decline in hours that took place. This is most obviously the case for
female employees: full-time hours showed little change in this period, but
the influx of mostly female part-timers undoubtedly reduced the average of
all female hours considerably.

Finally, the data are not adjusted for vacations and holidays, but these
are substantial in the United Kingdom and have grown significantly in the
last forty years. Only a small minority of British workers had paid vacations before World War II, according to Paul Blyton, and even as late as
the mid-fifties, a paid vacation "of less than two weeks was the norm for
almost all manual workers in Britain."[12] But government statistics indi-

cate that by 1960 vacation time had risen to ten days per year for these workers and that annual holidays stood at six. By 1986, the average manual worker enjoyed twenty-three days of vacation and eight holidays, for a total of thirty-one days per year.[13]

Hence, while the data for the United Kingdom are not as complete as they are for Germany, the available evidence indicates that here, too, significant reductions in the workweek occurred in the post–World War II period and that vacation and holiday time has more than doubled in the past twenty-five years.

Appendix to Chapter 2

The weekly working hours in Germany charted in figure 2.1 break down as follows:

Year	All	Male	Female	Year	All	Male	Female
1953	47.8	48.9	44.1	1973	42.8	43.3	38.9
1958	45.4	46.4	42.1	1978	41.6	42.1	39.6
1963	44.3	45.2	40.9	1983	40.5	40.8	39.1
1968	43.8	44.1	40.2	1985	40.7	40.9	39.5
				1986	40.4	40.8	39.2

Figure 2.2, presenting weekly working hours in France (establishment data), represents the following yearly estimates:

Year	All	Male	Female	Year	All	Male	Female
1946	44.0			1970	44.7		
1950	45.0			1975	42.1		
1955	45.3			1980	40.5		
1960	45.7			1982	39.4		
1965	45.6			1984	40.0	42.4	36.7
				1985	39.6	42.1	36.3

The hours worked per week by French employees charted in figure 2.3 (household survey data) were as follows: 1970, 44.7; 1975, 42.1; 1980, 40.5; 1986, 39.2.

The United States and Western Europe:
A Comparison

INTERNATIONAL COMPARISONS of work time are very difficult, even more difficult than an analysis of working hours in a single country. Each country collects, analyzes, and presents its data differently. Moreover, there are differences in customs and laws that influence work time, which sometimes make it difficult to analyze patterns.[1] Nevertheless, the data presented here do indicate that work time has been reduced more rapidly in Europe than in the United States since World War II.

Moreover, while the earlier part of the postwar period could be seen as one in which the Europeans were catching up with the Americans, who had led in obtaining a forty-hour workweek, the later period appears to be one in which the various European countries have moved ahead of the United States. For example, much greater progress in Western Europe—including Germany, France, and the United Kingdom—has been made in the 1980s in breaking the forty-hour barrier for full-time male workers. But the most dramatic example of the disparity between Europe and the United States is in annual days of paid leave: compare the U.S. average of 19.5 paid days leave a year (which includes sick time as well as vacations and holidays) with the 53.3 days enjoyed by the West German worker—almost three times as much!

There are a number of plausible explanations for the differences in working hours in the United States and in Western Europe. None is completely satisfactory, but together they may help us to understand why the two continents have followed different paths.

The most obvious explanation is the catching up theory. If the typical European employee had a workweek of about forty-eight hours at the end of World War II and the typical American one of not much more than forty hours, one can argue that the reason Europeans reduced hours more quickly is that the difficulties imposed from going from a forty-eight- to a forty-hour week are far less than those imposed as one reduces the workweek from forty to thirty-two hours. Indeed, a case can be made that workweek reduction becomes progressively more difficult for full-time workers as the workweek is reduced. (This argument—essentially, that the costs of further work time reduction to employers become larger and the benefits to employees smaller as the workweek becomes shorter—is discussed in detail in part 3.)

Certainly, resistance to reduction in Europe and in the United States becomes much more stubborn when the forty-hour threshold is reached. However, the catching up theory does not explain the much more successful assault on the forty-hour barrier in Europe in the past several years. Legal reduction of the standard workweek to thirty-nine hours occurred in France in 1982. In the following five years, trade unions in Germany, the United Kingdom, and indeed throughout Europe have fought for, and in a number of cases won, standard workweeks of thirty-five to thirty-nine hours. In addition, stricter controls on overtime have been written into legislation and union contracts, so as to narrow the gap between actual and standard hours for full-time employees. Large-scale programs to encourage the use of short time rather than layoffs have been in effect in a number of European countries for years and act to reduce the actual number of hours. Most recently, several European countries have enacted legislation to encourage employers to create more part-time jobs, especially for young people. All this effort to shorten the workweek to less than forty hours cannot be explained by the catching up theory.

Another explanation (rarely offered but of considerable promise) derives from welfare state legislation in Europe. Tax rates on effort are higher and social benefits provided by government much greater. Neoclassical economic theory would predict that the American worker, with a lower tax on his work but with the knowledge that the education of his children, his retirement income, and the medical needs of his entire family are largely dependent upon his own earnings, would be likely to offer more labor in the market.

True, the collective nature of much decision-making on working hours in Europe argues that the need for funds for this welfare state expenditure should condition the debate. But when this point is made at all by Europeans, they go on to deplore the relative lack of understanding of the argument by unions and other advocates of work time reduction. Thus, in a recent review of work time in Germany, Axel Weber of the IAB says that "the desire to exchange income for more leisure time may be favored by the high tax burden since the latter reduces the value of leisure time by reducing the losses in the net income considerably less than in the gross income. *It is often forgotten that the state and the social insurance are thus losing money*" (emphasis added).[2]

A third explanation of more rapid European hours reduction lies in the higher rate of growth in real wages there. Certainly, wage increases, and the productivity growth that makes real wage growth possible, have been rapid in Europe. For example, output per hour in both France and Germany rose from 1960 to 1980 at a rate twice that of the United States: the total rise over the twenty-year period increased productivity 70 percent relative to that in the United States. Even in the United Kingdom, output rose at a rate a third again as high as in the United States. Moreover, in many European countries, real wages rose even faster than productivity. In the United States, a further complication was that much of the modest gain made by American workers since 1970 has been taken in the form of increased premiums paid for health insurance, Social Security, private pension schemes, and the like. Real spendable earnings per hour have shown only small growth. Under these circumstances, a substantial reduction in annual work time would involve some very difficult choices for American workers. In contrast, a higher growth rate in Europe has meant that substantial reductions in work time could be made while living standards continued to increase.

A fourth explanation is that Europeans have reduced their work time because they have a greater taste for leisure—that, after all the economic determinants are taken into account or held constant, Europeans want more leisure than Americans do. This view has roots in the different history and tradition of the two continents and should not be dismissed lightly. At first glance, the course of hours reduction in Europe and the United States would appear to contradict this hypothesis, since, according to some observers, work time was on the average greater in Europe than in the United States during much of the late nineteenth and early twentieth century, and, as noted above, the forty-hour workweek was achieved first in America. Wages were much higher in the United States in this era, and that could explain such differences. But now that real wages are approaching parity in the two continents, Europeans are in advance of Americans in providing leisure for workers.

It is perhaps more difficult to explain international differences in the distribution of leisure—specifically, the European pattern of increasing vacation days and holidays well above those in the United States long before weekly hours in Europe had fallen to the U.S. level. There are, of course, cultural explanations for this difference. One such was offered by an internationally recognized expert on vacation time in Europe as well as in the United States (an economist at the IAB in Nuremberg).

In his view, the stronger preference for long vacations in Germany than in the United States derives from the pressure of everyday living in an overcrowded European country. Contributing factors include the German ethic of high-quality work on the job and the rigid closing times of retail establishments, which make shopping much more difficult for the employed consumer than it is in the United States. Commuting problems in some areas also contribute to these pressures. For all these reasons, the argument runs, the German worker needs a complete change in his environment once a year to maintain his equilibrium. Evaluation of this cultural explanation (like the more developed taste for leisure) raises questions far beyond the economist's sphere, and these will not be pursued here.

Increases in vacation time can be explained in a more pragmatic way, however, on the basis of the manner in which vacation time is established in Europe and in the United States. In France, minimum vacation days have been set by the national government since 1936. In Germany, unions determine vacations—as well as wages, hours, and other benefits—for nonunion workers as well as union members in each industry. Moreover, the trade unions are closely identified with the Social Democratic Party, one of Germany's two principal political parties. As a result, social concerns—or at least voters' preferences—are considered in the determination of vacations, hours, and other labor benefits. In the United Kingdom, a much higher proportion of the labor force is organized than in the United States, and labor unions are closely tied to the British Labour Party.

In contrast, there is no law requiring any vacations at all for workers in the United States. Moreover, four-fifths of the U.S. labor force is not in trade unions, and in any case U.S. unions are not formally affiliated with a political party. Hence the concerns of the individual employer, employee, or union—rather than social concerns—have been paramount in the design of benefits. Vacations have traditionally been seen by U.S. employers as a reward for long service, affording rest and reducing the burnout problem for senior employees. At the same time, the promise of future vacation time is thought to tie employees to the company and so to reduce turnover.[3]

Vacations and holidays in Europe are based on the view that society has an obligation to provide an annual vacation of a decent length even to young workers. They also take into account the more pragmatic social argument that generous leave for youthful blue collar workers who have successfully completed one year of continuous employment eases the transition from school to work and so reduces problems of absenteeism and quits—and hence unemployment, with its known social costs. This emphasis on social rather than individual considerations thus helps to explain why Europeans have had more success than Americans in crossing the threshold of the forty-hour workweek.

PART II

Medium-Term Effects of Reduced Work Time

CHAPTER FOUR

Arguments for Government Intervention

SHOULD the United States follow the example of Europe and give a greater role to collective decision making in determining the pace of work time reduction? In Europe, the two major factors operating in the collective process are trade unions and government. In the United States, the trade union movement does not now appear to be in a position to demand and obtain significant hours reductions. This country does, however, have the option of using government: the most obvious way to accelerate work time reduction in the United States, and so narrow the gap between hours in America and Europe, is through legislation.

This chapter considers a variety of arguments that have been made by economists and others for such legislation. The first part presents a brief historical summary of arguments used in support of legislation to reduce hours to forty per week. The second part sets forth an argument currently used for a legislated reduction below the forty-hour level: that it would create jobs. This has become the principal argument (especially in Europe) for further work time reduction through legislation.

Early Arguments

There is a long history of effort to obtain legislation to reduce the work-week, efforts that culminated in the passage of the Fair Labor Standards Act in 1940. A variety of arguments were developed in the course of this struggle, which can be divided into three general categories, based on the following propositions: first, that the labor market is in some way imperfect and so does not itself produce optimal results; second, that a reduction in hours improves the lot of the worker relative to the owners of capital and other more affluent members of society and so provides a less unequal distribution of income; and third, that a reduction in hours helps the economy to maintain higher output and lower unemployment and to provide other macroeconomic benefits. Arguments based on each of these three propositions are considered below.[1]

MARKET FAILURE

Some economists accepted the popular view that long hours of work should be prohibited in order to protect the health of the worker.[2] It was argued that even if workers could always set their own work times, the state should still intervene because many workers prefer to work longer than is best for society: that is, they discount the future more heavily than is good for society and so are too willing to sacrifice their future health and productivity for current income and consumption.[3] Other reasons for accepting the health argument for regulation include the supposedly invincible ignorance of workers on the long-term damage to their health of long hours, and the externality argument: that much of the future cost of illness and lost productivity will be borne by the state, so that the latter has a right to influence work time.

Yet another reason for rejecting the effects of a free-market outcome on health is based on a critique of the *processes* that set hours. In practice, individual workers typically cannot determine their schedules. And while a simple version of economic theory predicts that competition is likely to ensure the mix of hours and weekly wages that is most acceptable to the average employee, a number of economists have pointed out over the years that a range of wages and hours is more likely under more realistic circumstances (as when there is imperfect information about employment alternatives). In the absence of unions, the employer is then said to have greater bargaining power over the actual terms of the wages and hours that occur in this less determinate situation. Moreover, the bargaining power of the employee is said to be greater over hours than over wages, since wages can be individually negotiated, but a standard hours schedule is offered to the employee on a take-it-or-leave-it basis. Hence hours decisions will be more skewed to the employer's interest.[4] Some critics of labor market processes have used this argument to advocate government intervention to restore a balance by regulating hours, especially when long hours imperil health.[5]

Health ceased to be widely used as an argument for reducing the standard workweek once the forty-hour week was achieved, but it still has some applicability as an argument for reducing overtime (and overtime reduction is, after all, one way of reducing work time). In the American legal system, hours of overtime are at the employer's discretion—he is obligated only to pay a time-and-a-half premium—and under some circumstances (discussed in the next chapter) it will pay the employer to offer many hours of overtime. By contrast, legal limits on the total number of hours worked per week are common in European countries.[6] In the event that similar legislation is considered in the United States at some future time, the health argument for hours regulation would be relevant, even with the forty-hour standard workweek. (It will not, however, be considered at further length here.)

The effects of work schedules on family life have also been used to justify government intervention on social grounds. If the head of the family undervalued the utility of other family members and preferred to put in long hours to provide consumption goods for himself, then a social interest in family life—not captured in free-market outcomes—could be invoked to justify restriction. Effects of long hours on family life were given a major role in the effort to reduce work time in Germany in the 1950s. Then, the rallying cry of the unions seeking to move from a six- to a five-day week was, "Saturday, Daddy belongs with us." Family structures have changed in the past thirty years, and the family argument for hours reduction has changed accordingly. On both sides of the Atlantic, hours reduction is sometimes advocated on the grounds that it will permit a more equal distribution of market employment between husbands and wives.

The popularity of arguments in favor of reducing hours on health or family grounds may reflect an unwillingness to acknowledge the economic cost to the worker of hours reduction. For example, it becomes more difficult to make the health argument for hours reduction under semisubsistence conditions if one reasons that a reduction in the hours of a worker employed at an hourly rate near subsistence level will, by lowering weekly earnings, impose serious deficiencies in the nutrition, housing, and clothing of the whole family.[7] Similarly, those who under more affluent, modern conditions argue that some parents will work excessive hours, sacrificing time with their families in order to obtain more consumer goods, would have to recognize that there are other parents who prefer to work very little, even if this means substandard living conditions for their families.

One reason for the lack of recognition of the full economic costs of hours reduction is that at the firm or industry level hours reduction is sometimes accompanied by an increase in hourly pay rates. If the resulting cost increase can be passed on to other members of society (in the form of lower profits for shareholders or higher prices for consumers), the economic cost to the workers is minimized. Favorable outcomes at this microlevel can give rise to an overly optimistic appraisal of the effects of a reduction in hours for all members of the labor force.[8] (Compare the more detailed discussion of this point in part 3.)

More recently, the energy crisis of the 1970s gave rise to yet another set of market failure arguments for hours reduction. The underlying premise of these arguments was that the market process—for example, higher prices for gasoline and other petroleum products—did not sufficiently curtail energy consumption or increase supply. Shorter hours—especially if they were scheduled over fewer working days—would help to save energy and so would be an alternative to layoffs. A reduction in commuting trips would be an obvious benefit. Reduced use of heating and lighting in offices and of power sources in factories would bring further gains. And if hours reduction yielded a cut in the living standards of the American people, this was good also, since (according to a popular theory among journalists in the late seventies) we had brought about the energy crisis by overexploiting the earth's resources in order to sustain an artificial and extravagant lifestyle. Such arguments are less popular today. (A critique of the argument that hours reduction is a useful way of dealing with energy and materials supply problems is presented in chapter 13.)

REDISTRIBUTION

Hours reduction has also been advocated on the grounds that it will improve the *economic* condition of the working class, with concomitant benefits for society. This too is an old argument. The first American labor party argued in the 1840s that active participation of an educated working class was necessary if our political democracy was to deliver economic and other rewards to working men and women. But this required leisure: time to study the issues and time to take part in the political process. And such leisure was not available to workers on the very long work schedules then in place.

Later in the nineteenth century, Ira Steward, George Gunton, and other leading advocates of the eight-hour day argued that a reduction in daily hours would increase not only hourly but daily wages.[9] The argument of Steward and his many followers was based on a once popular theory of wage determination. Daily or weekly wages were said to be set by the minimum requirements or living standards of the workers. This theory had a number of applications. For example, the importation of laborers from a country where workers lived at a low standard was believed to reduce wages because the immigrants could live on less than Americans. But if wages could be lowered by bringing in workers with lower living standards than Americans, they could be raised by increasing the living standards of Americans. And this could be done by reducing hours of work.

As Cahill summarizes the Steward argument, "Decreased hours, through giving the worker time to observe the mode of living of other people, and to carry on a social life, would increase wants. The result of these increased wants would be a successful demand for higher wages; therefore, Steward posited that the first step away from poverty must come by a reduction of hours."[10] This analysis provided a quite popular argument for hours reduction among unionists and other labor supporters.

A third theory that supported the wage-increasing properties of hours reduction was the labor scarcity argument. If you wish to raise the price of a good or service, you reduce its supply to the market. On this rather conventional reasoning, a reduction in hours will tend to increase hourly wages.[11]

Greatly increased leisure for American male workers has tended to make obsolete the first of these microeconomic arguments, and the wage theory that supported the second theory has itself become obsolete.[12] However, the third argument is based on a more modern supply and demand theory of wage determination. It is still offered today, though few economists believe that the demand for labor is so inelastic that a reduction in its supply, by reducing hours, would increase hourly wages to the point that weekly income, in real terms, is increased. On the contrary, estimates of the demand for labor generally predict that a decrease in living standards will result. (Compare the discussion of this point in later chapters, especially chapters 8 and 12.)

MACROECONOMIC BENEFIT

Hours reduction policy has often been advocated because of its perceived macroeconomic benefits. It is said that long hours of work leave the worker with insufficient time to consume the products he made or to develop the sophisticated tastes to demand them. This argument seemed plausible to many in the years of industrialization in the United States, when hours were still relatively long and when the industrial production of consumer goods was rising rapidly. It was taken up in the 1920s by Henry Ford, a pioneer of the forty-hour workweek in his own factories.[13] The complex products available in the decade after World War I did seem to require more leisure to use them. In the 1900–1920 period, movies, records, and other inventions had already helped to achieve a reduction in hours, to forty-eight to fifty-four hours a week for many workers.[14] But the innovations associated with the automobile culture apparently required further gains in leisure time—two days off per week, instead of one.

In more recent years, some have continued to argue for a relation between leisure and spending and have charted the growth of the recreation, restaurant, and other leisure-oriented industries, as vacations, holidays, and long weekends have increased. Some still believe that an increase in leisure would stimulate consumer spending and so give a boost to the economy. However, these arguments are not widely accepted today. The case rests on two propositions that are now considered dubious: that Americans do not consume enough of their income and that reductions in hours of work will raise the proportion of income consumed. Few economists today accept a naive underconsumptionist explanation of unemployment—the savings rate is not high, by historical standards, and many believe that an increase in savings would be beneficial. And, in any event, there is no em-

pirical evidence that an increase in leisure would in itself affect the proportion of income consumed.[15]

This critique need not imply that the earlier consumption-leisure argument was wrong. It may simply have lost relevance once the forty-hour
week had been achieved. Thus, over thirty years ago Herbert Northrup and
Herbert Brinberg wrote: "We are not dealing here with the twelve-hour
day, but rather with the eight-hour day and the forty-hour week. Since the
average worker spends the bulk of his income on consumption, it may well
be that he is about as good a customer for the nonessential items of industrial production as can be expected."[16]

The economic collapse of the 1930s gave a new importance to macroeconomic arguments for hours reduction. Advocates relied heavily on the
work-sharing theory (discussed below), that a shorter workweek would
provide a more equitable distribution of the costs of a shrunken demand
for labor. But some also argued that a forty-hour workweek would raise
output by speeding economic recovery: work sharing was seen as having
two beneficial effects. It would maintain purchasing power among a wide
base of workers and so stabilize the retail trade and financial industries;
and it would also put a floor under hourly wage rates (which were declining
in the early thirties) by helping workers resist wage cuts, thus limiting de-
flationary expectations, and so further stabilizing the economy. This
Keynesian-type analysis may have had some validity for the economic condition of the 1930s, but its applicability to the problem of reducing unemployment in the 1980s is questioned by many economists. (Compare the
discussion of macroeconomic effects in chapter 9.)

The Modern Case for Work Sharing

In recent years, the principal argument in favor of legislation to reduce
work time has been that it will spread available work, thus reducing unemployment and causing a number of socially desirable effects. This argument has been well received in Western Europe, where the oil shocks of
1973 and 1979 and the much higher unemployment rates in subsequent
years put work time reduction high on the agendas of many European
trade unions and governments.

The increased interest in work sharing has in fact changed the way in
which Europeans have approached work time reduction: more attention is
now given to unemployment considerations, less to other arguments. This
shift is described in a recent report by Axel Weber of the German Ministry
for Labor and Social Affairs to the International Institute of Labour. In
Germany, "up to the time when the 40 hours week was realized, reduction
of collectively agreed weekly working time was the most important

issue. . . . The question of the redistribution of work was . . . not an issue at that time."[17] According to Weber, this thinking characterized the fifties and sixties, when unemployment was low and the rate of growth in real hourly wages was high. In the seventies, unemployment rose, growth slowed, and work time reduction largely took the form of cuts in overtime and increases in part-time work. But there was an important change in the eighties as unemployment rates rose still further. As Weber pointed out, "Recently the opinion has gained ground that in the medium-term without reducing working time unemployment cannot be brought down sufficiently. Now the controversial question is primarily how and not whether the working time should be reduced."[18] A similar analysis could be offered, with modifications, for a number of European countries.

PROSPECTS IN THE UNITED STATES

A key issue in considering the future of work time in the United States is whether it should follow this European example. Work time legislation does not have a high priority in the United States at the present time, when unemployment is comparatively low. But this could change. One can readily construct a plausible scenario for higher unemployment in the next several years, and a number of writers have done so. Those who do predict large-scale unemployment and a consequent increase in interest in work-sharing legislation can point to several factors in support of their arguments. First, the present upward movement in economic activity has been extremely long-lived by historical standards. Many observers believe that a downturn in the late eighties is overdue.

Second, a number of recent economic developments can be interpreted as predicting an economic downturn. These include a corporate debt-equity ratio that is high by historical standards (low corporate liquidity is said to make the economy especially vulnerable); large amounts of U.S. debt—private and public—held by foreigners (also said to be a source of instability); and a precarious international economy, characterized by a large U.S. trade deficit, high foreign debts owed by a number of countries, and an increase in protectionist sentiments in much of the industrialized world. Economists, business journalists, and others who project a severe economic setback regard the October 1987 stock market crash as a significant omen.

If a recession or depression does occur, few doubt that a serious increase in unemployment would ensue. There has been a long-term upward movement in peak unemployment over the various cycles since the end of World War II. A severe setback could, in principle, lead to unemployment rates in the double-digit range. This would almost certainly yield demands for work-sharing legislation, and there are several reasons for believing that these might be successful. First, the country is (according to some political observers) once again ready to expand the role of government in resolving social issues. Second, work-sharing policy has been tried extensively in Europe, and there is a tradition in the United States to look to Europe for innovative welfare state or labor legislation. Third, the very fact that the legislated standard workweek in the United States has not been changed for almost fifty years makes it an attractive target for some reformers. And, finally, some positive steps have actually been taken by government (admittedly on a very modest scale) to encourage work sharing in the United States in the past several years, indicating a receptivity to this policy. (These efforts are discussed below.)

The above is presented as a plausible scenario, not as a forecast. But if a strong campaign for work-sharing legislation is even a plausible event, it behooves us now to consider carefully the efficacy of work time reduction as a means of creating jobs, or of serving other social ends. It would be unfortunate if such reasoned discussion were postponed until unemployment was high and political interests were engaged. The next several chapters endeavor to analyze the work-sharing argument in some detail. In this discussion, the European experience with work sharing as well as the debate that this experience has generated are examined in the hope that some light will be shed on whether the United States should follow the European example.

EMPLOYMENT EFFECTS

In considering employment and other effects of work time reduction it is important to distinguish between short-, medium-, and long-term policies. The short run is used here to denote a period extending over a phase of a business cycle or fluctuation, the recession or the recovery, or at most the cycle itself. On the other hand, the long run denotes a period long enough for the full effects of hours reduction to have occurred. These effects include an adjustment in capital stock and even changes in the educational system (and thus adjustments in human capital). Hence, this period extends over many years. The medium run is a period of intermediate duration. It lasts for more than one cycle in economic activity. But while it is long enough for changes in the capital stock and in other long-term impact areas to have begun, it is not sufficiently long for these impact variables to be fully adjusted to a new level of working hours.

The discussion in part 2 concentrates on medium-term work-sharing effects. The long-term argument for reducing hours to spread work opportunities is weak, although a number of other important economic and social effects of a permanent work time reduction are likely, and these are considered in detail in part 3. A good case can also be made for encouraging short-run fluctuations in hours—that is, for a policy that encourages employers to reduce hours of work per employee as the economy moves into a recession and then to increase hours as economic conditions recover. Employers have long done just this without government intervention: reducing overtime and setting short-time schedules when conditions warrant it.

Indeed, a recent study by Martin Nemirow found that fifty years ago employers absorbed a larger fraction of fluctuations in their demand for labor through hours variation and a smaller fraction through employment changes than they do today.[19] Many would like to see this trend reversed and more use made of hours fluctuations. Insofar as hours fluctuations do in fact reduce the volatility of employment, some clear advantages can be seen in a short-term work-sharing policy. Unemployment causes distress to individual workers and their families. It is said to increase indexes of psychological stress such as suicide and divorce rates. Higher unemployment also affects the rest of society in a variety of ways, imposing costs not only on the unemployment system but also on the welfare system, including Medicaid, and on law enforcement.

A related advantage of cyclical work sharing is that it is said to produce a fairer distribution of working hours lost in an economic downturn by spreading this cost over a larger number of people. Moreover, since the seniority system of layoffs is now established in much of the economy, layoffs tend to be concentrated among relatively new hires, and today these are often the young, women, and members of ethnic minorities. Work sharing is said to shift some of the cost of a recession from these new groups to older workers. Of course, not all workers agree that this change is desirable. The older worker has spent years under risk of layoff (and possibly has been laid off a number of times) in order to acquire precious seniority. To such workers, equity might require that new employees serve the same apprenticeship of insecurity that they did themselves.

Nevertheless, many writers have pointed out the social advantages of work sharing when it is initiated at the level of the individual firm. A recent study by Jocelyn Gutchess showed how private corporations can use variations in hours as one of several tools to minimize employment fluctuations.[20] It is worth noting that the policy recommended was not one of simply reducing hours to create jobs. Instead, it called for a program of cyclical work sharing: raising hours and minimizing new hires during a period of temporary expansion. Hours would then be cut and layoffs minimized or avoided altogether when demand for the firm's products fell.

The case is not so strong for legislative action to compel cyclical work sharing, for two reasons. In the first place, it is often easier to force firms to reduce the hours of their workers than it is to induce them to hire new workers to replace lost hours. This issue is considered in some detail in the discussion of the employment effects of medium-term hours reduction in the next five chapters. In the second place, legislation is a cumbersome tool to deal with a short-term need for work sharing: before jobs can be saved, the need for corrective action must be recognized. Congress and the executive must act, and the policy must be implemented. Because there are lags in all three processes, the legislative procedure is less effective in dealing with short-term cycles than in correcting medium- or long-term difficulties.

These objections do not apply to one important legislative initiative: reform of the unemployment insurance system. In the United States, this system has biased employers against using hours fluctuations, since the system provides a net subsidy to employers who lay off workers but not to those who use hours fluctuations.[21] An effort has now been made in eleven states to correct for this bias by introducing short-time compensation schemes, which permit workers temporarily on short schedules to receive a portion of their unemployment benefits equal to the fraction by which their hours have been reduced. Similar schemes have been employed in Western Europe for many years and may help to account for the greater use of hours fluctuations there.[22]

A revised unemployment system has the advantage in that it simply encourages hours reduction and so is less likely to induce the evasive responses by employers that one expects from compulsion (considered in the next chapter). Moreover, the policy operates automatically as the firm's demand declines: there need not be any lags in its application.

The principal focus of this study, though, is not fluctuations in hours per worker but, rather, longer lasting reductions in hours. This distinction is especially pertinent to the interpretation of the current work-sharing debate. Europeans have been enacting permanent reductions, reducing hours without any provision for increasing them at some future time. Moreover, this policy is not adopted in response to a temporary downturn, however severe, but rather to what is regarded as a persistent unemployment crisis. Unemployment rates have remained relatively high for over a decade, and Europeans generally do not foresee a return to lower rates in the near future. Such medium-term considerations have shaped the entire work-sharing debate in Europe.

WORK-SHARING PLANS IN EUROPE

One reason many Europeans turned to work sharing is that they did not see ready alternative solutions to their economic difficulties. A number of factors contributed to this pessimistic outlook. Some analysts attribute employment stagnation to the fact that in European countries the majority of the nonagricultural work force is typically unionized and wages are tightly controlled throughout the economy, making it difficult for wages to fall to market-clearing levels. And a rigid wage structure is said both to accelerate the rate at which jobs are eliminated in the declining sector and to slow down the rate at which they are created in the growing sector.

A complementary explanation of European stagnation notes that economic theory also predicts that structural unemployment will be exacerbated if the state provides generous support for the unemployed, through unemployment and welfare benefits. This is an especially important factor today, when the unemployed have to make painful sacrifices to find jobs. A move from manufacturing to the service sector may involve a substantial reduction in pay and status. It may also require an investment by the worker in training or in a move to another part of the country. The interaction of these contemporary conditions with the generous welfare state programs for the unemployed in most European countries is predicted to yield long delays before a worker is reemployed.

Dealing with these structural problems is also more difficult if governments are constrained to follow restrictive monetary and other macroeconomic policies. Fear of inflation and of a fall in the value of the nation's currency may lead policymakers to create an environment in which job growth is limited. Inasmuch as there is considerable disagreement as to the mix of policies that will maximize employment (since an overly expansive policy can also yield a decline in employment), it is sometimes difficult to say when a country's restrictive policies are in fact inhibiting employment growth. However, there is a widespread perception that this has been the case in a number of European countries. Under these circumstances, it is easy to understand why many Europeans have been pessimistic about the possibility of stimulating a satisfactory growth in employment, at least in the medium term. It is also easy to see why such pessimism has made the idea of work sharing more attractive: it has been seen as a way of dividing an apparently fixed amount of work among a larger number of people.

The European economic planner who has adopted the work-sharing philosophy begins to implement it by making a series of forecasts: of international demand for national exports, of the cost and availability of imported fuels and other raw materials, and of various domestic constraints. These predictions enable the planner to forecast national output over some planning period. On the basis of past trends in output per hour, the planner then projects national demand for labor. Labor supply is forecast by considering the numbers who reach the usual age of entrance into the labor force, the trend in female labor force participation, and the trend in the participation of older people. Subtraction of expected labor demand from expected labor supply shows an excess supply, which leads the planner to predict intolerably high unemployment. The planner then concludes that some combination of hours reduction and increased retirements should be considered as a way to ration jobs.

Before recommending a workweek reduction, direct and other labor market effects are considered. How many workers would be affected by the new law? How well would it be enforced? Would it increase the number of those seeking part-time or other moonlighting opportunities? Would it increase overtime? Would it increase the number of women looking for work? Would it raise output per hour, and hence limit the expected increase in employment? Would it be accompanied by a compensating increase in hourly wages? Would this yield a net increase in unit labor costs? Would capital capacity be underutilized (unless offset by increased shift work)? Special problems in industries that require a twenty-four-hour-a-day operation are also considered, often with considerable sophistication.

The planner then attempts to predict the indirect effects of hours reduction, using the techniques of macroeconomics. Assumptions about the various direct effects of workweek reduction are entered into a macroeconomic model, and the simulation technique is used to predict the effect of this policy on a wide range of macroeconomic variables, including employment and unemployment. On the basis of some optimistic assumptions about macro- and microeconomic effects of hours reduction on the economy, the government would then set forth a plan for work sharing.

The above is a good description of government thinking in several countries in the late seventies and early eighties. But recent experience has caused some European policymakers to revise their approach to hours reduction and to adopt a more skeptical view of the work-sharing remedy. It has also generated a vigorous intellectual debate in which a number of European economists have made important contributions to our understanding of work-sharing policy. They have often come up with a negative assessment of its efficiency.

The following chapters consider in more detail the principal economic assumptions that underlie the work-sharing argument and endeavor to explain the increased skepticism among economists and others about the proposition that government policies designed to reduce working hours yield higher employment—and so could be properly described as work sharing.

CHAPTER FIVE

Offsets to Government Intervention

> In the last analysis, it is by this difficulty—the final impossibility of preventing evasion—that Trade Unions and Wage Boards, like almost all systems of economic regulation since the dawn of history, are defeated. Capitalist enterprise is the child of evasion; and on the long road from ancient smuggler to modern industrialist, the entrepreneur has learned more tricks than are easily reckoned with.
>
> —Hicks, "Hours and Conditions," in *The Theory of Wages*

THE FIRST QUESTION to ask of a policy to reduce work time is whether it actually does reduce it. This question has attracted considerable attention from economists, but their analysis indicates that it is not an easy one to answer.

Evasions and Exemptions

One reason that the actual effect of legislation is likely to be less than that intended is lack of enforcement. It is well known that in the United States many laws, including labor laws, are not effectively enforced. Some companies endeavor to evade the law when evasion is consistent with profit maximization. But evasion becomes unprofitable only when the taxpayers are willing to pay for an adequate enforcement effort, and such commitment is often not forthcoming for labor legislation in the United States.

Orley Ashenfelter found that there was widespread evasion of the Fair Labor Standards Act, the legislation that provides the principal legal constraints within which hours and wages are determined in the United States. Ashenfelter estimated that fewer than two-thirds of affected employers complied with the minimum wage provision of the act.[1] In a careful study of noncompliance with the overtime provisions of the FLSA, Ronald Ehrenberg and Paul Schuman concluded that the data "suggest that at least 10 to 20 percent of the employees working overtime who should legally receive a premium of time and a half for overtime fail to receive it."[2]

In addition, the FLSA allows exemptions. In 1978, only 59 percent of wage and salary workers were covered by the overtime provisions of the act.

As a result of evasions and exemptions, only 43 percent of employees who work overtime were paid for it. Moreover, this overestimates the effect of the federal legislation, since uncovered workers receive benefits for other reasons: because of clauses in their union contracts; because they are employees of state and local governments, which are exempt from federal legislation but which have their own provisions for overtime; or because they work for private employers who voluntarily pay overtime benefits. For example, a study by Fred Best found that 65 percent of all workers receiving overtime premiums in 1978 were among the roughly 21 percent of the American labor force that is unionized, giving support to those who relate overtime payment to union status.[3] If an attempt were made to change hours by law to a level well below that sought by both employers and employees, one would see a sharp increase in incentives for employers to violate the law, and hence one could predict an increase in violations above those found in previous studies.

Increased Overtime Expectations

REDUCTIONS IN HOURLY WAGES

A more subtle form of avoidance of the effects of lowering the legal standard for working hours occurs when employers are in a position to set hourly wages as well as hours. They can then maintain the status quo, despite the change in the hours standard. Consider a firm that has been paying $400 for a forty-hour workweek. If the standard workweek is reduced to thirty-five hours, the firm now must pay time and a half for the last five hours of work. But if the firm just reduces the hourly base rate by 6 percent, weekly earnings are unchanged. (The worker now earns $9.41 an hour for the first thirty-five hours and $14.12 for the last five hours, for a total of $400.) If the law is more strict and requires payment of double time for overtime, the firm can still maintain the original conditions if it can reduce hourly wages by 12 percent.

It can be shown that in theory this result obtains under a variety of assumptions about employer and employee attitudes toward schedules. For example, the firm might prefer longer (or shorter) hours if these were available at a constant wage rate, while employees may prefer shorter (or longer) schedules, on the same assumption. But if the initial conditions ($400 for forty hours of work, in this example) represent the competitive labor market outcome for the profit-maximizing firm—that is, the result of rather complex calculations of the production gains and labor costs of different schedules and of their effects on the preferences of its employees (and hence on its personnel costs)—the firm would have no incentive to reduce hours. It would be better off if it cut hourly wages, maintained weekly hours and earnings, and so evaded the effect of the new hours law.

In practice, though, employers typically do not have unlimited freedom to set hourly wages. In the first place, the FLSA specifically prohibits reducing hourly wages below the rate paid before the law went into effect. It is likely that a new reduction in the standard workweek would be accompanied by a similar prohibition. In the second place, even without the FLSA, employers have found it difficult to reduce money wages for a number of reasons: union contracts; individual contracts; civil service and other government regulations; and, more generally, concern about the morale and reputational effects for the firm if it becomes known as a wage cutter. (In the next chapter, some reasons are given for actually expecting an increase in money wages as hours are reduced.)

However, some firms can at least hold money hourly wages constant. Then, even at a moderate rate of inflation, real wages can be reduced by the required amount (6 percent in this example) rather quickly. And economic theory predicts that the hours chosen by the firm would be determined by real, not monetary, wages. (The theory holds that the firm, in deciding how much labor to hire, is comparing the money wages it must pay to the price it obtains for its product, while employees' preferences for work time are determined by a comparison of their wages with the prices of the consumer goods they purchase. Hence, a proportional increase in all wages and prices should not affect matters.) According to this theory, then, a freeze on money wages would permit the firm to return to the status quo in real terms—hours and real weekly earnings—within a comparatively short period.

HIGHER FRINGE BENEFITS

Another factor reducing the effect of hours legislation is that overtime premium rates do not apply to many fringe benefits, and this tends to reduce the efficacy of a reduction in the standard workweek. The U.S. Chamber of Commerce estimates that fringe benefits now constitute about a third of total compensation for employees in U.S. manufacturing.

Since many of these fringe benefits do not increase at all with overtime, the employer has an incentive to increase hours of work. In fact, it can be shown that if fixed fringe benefits account for over a third of total compensation, then, even with provisions for time-and-a-half payment for overtime, average hourly compensation declines with hours worked. Consider a hypothetical example in which workers initially are paid $10 an hour for a forty-hour week and receive fixed fringe benefits of $200, for a total compensation of $600. Their average hourly compensation is $15. Extra hours of work are paid at the overtime rate of $15 an hour, so that their compensation rises to $750 for fifty hours, $900 for sixty hours, and so on. However, their average hourly compensation remains at $15. If the fixed benefits are higher than $200 here, average hourly compensation actually declines with longer hours of work.

Of course, this argument does not imply that the presence of fixed fringe benefits would negate the effect of introducing overtime premia. Without these penalty rates, average hourly compensation costs would decline with hours of work (because of the fixed fringe benefits), and employers would have an incentive to schedule long hours.[4] In our example, when extra hours are paid at straight time, average hourly compensation declines from $15 at forty hours to $14 at fifty hours and $12.50 at sixty hours. With the introduction of the overtime premia, the fringe benefit effect is offset.

However, it remains true that, *if the ratio of fringe benefits to wage payments rises as overtime premia are introduced,* the positive effect of the one can offset the negative effect of the other. And a number of observers have noted that something of the sort appears to have taken place: that in the decades subsequent to the passage of the Fair Labor Standards Act the proportion of fringe benefits in the typical employee's compensation package rose very sharply, negating much of the impact of the hours legislation.

One should not assume, though, that this trend necessarily demonstrates another form of employer evasion of the FLSA. Correlation need not indicate causation, and there is a wealth of evidence that the upward trend in fringe benefits resulted from many different factors. These benefits met deeply felt employee needs for pensions, health care, other insurance, vacations, and so on, as well as providing tax and other advantages to employers.

OVERTIME EFFECTS WITH CONSTANT HOURLY WAGES

A number of economists have argued that a legislated reduction in the standard workweek would *increase* hours of work, at least for those employees already working overtime. This argument was put forward by American economists in the sixties and early seventies[5] and has been taken up by a number of European participants in the work time debate of the eighties. Indeed, in recent years it has played a major role in the academic discussion of work sharing.[6]

In this analysis, hourly wages and fringe benefits are assumed to be fixed. The firm is assumed to seek to produce its output at a minimum labor cost (other things being equal). To produce the output, the firm requires a certain amount of labor services, or effective labor input. These labor services are a positive function of the number of employees and the number of hours per employee. Employees and hours are partial substitutes in production—substitutes in that the same amount of output can be produced with different combinations of employees and hours—but only partial substitutes, since diminishing returns may be encountered as increased numbers of employees are substituted for hours per employee, or vice versa.

The task of the employer, then, is to find the combination that minimizes his labor cost. If we assume that the firm is at this point before the hours law is changed—and will find a new cost-minimizing solution after it is revised—then we can simply ask how the change in the law will affect the cost-minimizing combination of employees and hours. A condition for cost minimization is that the ratio of the marginal production benefit of an additional employee to the marginal product of an additional hour per employee equals the ratio of the marginal cost of adding another employee to the marginal cost of increasing hours per employee by one.

A change in the hours law will not affect the production technology, but it will change costs. If employees are already working overtime, a reduction in the standard workweek will not change the cost of an extra hour per employee. If the overtime premium is one-half, the cost of an extra hour remains at one-and-a-half times the wage rate. But a change in the hours law *will* change the cost of hiring an additional employee. Again, on the assumption that employees are already on overtime, a reduction in the standard workweek will (if work time is unchanged) increase the amount of overtime pay employees receive and so increase the daily cost to the firm. For example, if employees work 9 hours a day and the law provides for time-and-a-half pay after 8 hours, their daily pay is 9.5 times their standard hourly rate. But if the law is changed so that overtime is paid after 7 hours, they are paid 10 times the hourly wage each day. Thus the cost of hiring an additional employee is, ceteris paribus, increased by a reduction in the standard workweek, on these assumptions. Since the cost of an additional hour per employee has remained the same and the cost of an additional employee has risen, employees have become dearer relative to hours, and the cost-minimizing employer has an incentive to substitute hours for employees, which is likely to yield a longer workday or workweek.[7]

It is easy to see the analytical appeal of this simple argument. However, one must be careful to assess it accurately. The paradox requires that overtime be worked before standard hours are reduced. It does not occur when hours are at or below standard. In the latter case, a reduction in the standard workweek will increase the marginal cost of an hour of work. For example, if the actual workday is 7.75 hours in the above example, a reduction in the standard workday from 8 to 7 hours means that the marginal cost to the employer of an extra hour of work per worker has increased by 50 percent. And in the United States (unlike some European countries), average hours are typically at or below the standard. Moreover, this analysis predicts that, if a reduction in the standard workweek is accompanied by an increase in the overtime premium, this paradoxical effect need not occur, even for those employees on overtime: their actual hours could also be reduced[8] (although the result would then be a remarkable increase in labor costs, which could in itself have a strongly negative effect on employment).

Finally, Tuire Santamaki-Vuori pointed out that the paradox is also avoided if one has a range of overtime premia—say, time and a half for the first five hours, double time for the next five, and so on.[9] Then, a reduction in the standard workweek automatically pushes some employees up into the next overtime rate level, and so raises the marginal cost of an extra hour of overtime for them. This automatic increase in the marginal overtime rate may give the employer an incentive to reduce his hours.[10] However, the law as it stands provides just a single standard premium, of 50 percent. And one of the principal reasons for demands for hours is that millions of employees work overtime, while others are out of work altogether.

Overtime: Empirical Evidence

The simplest way to determine whether legislation reducing the standard workweek will reduce actual hours of work would appear to be to observe whether these hours fall after the legislation is enacted. But in practice this method yields ambiguous results. The reduction called for by legislation is often small. And if there is also a downward time trend in hours—due to the workings of the private labor market—it is often difficult to determine whether any observed reduction in actual hours that occurs after the legislation is passed is a result of the policy or whether it would have occurred independently, as part of the market-based trend.

An interesting example is provided by recent French experience. The workweek of forty hours was reduced by law in 1982. According to the government's announced plan, hours would be cut by one per week each year until they reached thirty-five per week. But only the first installment was carried out, so that the workweek in France remains at thirty-nine hours. Under these circumstances, it has been extremely difficult to assess the impact of work time policy. True, an analysis of month-by-month movements in French hours does show the effect of the introduction of the new hours law—a relatively sharp drop in the following year. But reductions in subsequent years have been very slow. When one looks at the 1980–86 period as a whole, one finds a *slower* annual rate of decline than in previous years. (Compare the discussion of these data in chapter 2.) On the other hand, one cannot assume that the policy was altogether ineffective: after all, the forty-hour level has provided a psychological barrier to further reduction in many countries and industries, and the 1982 law did take France below that level. Similar questions must be raised about recent, highly publicized reductions in the workweek below the forty-hour level in other European countries. It will be interesting to see whether they are followed, in the years ahead, by significant additional reductions.

One can also question the impact of the Fair Labor Standards Act on the medium- or long-term trend of hours in the United States. The workweek was already near forty hours for the majority of covered workers when the act was passed. And, as we saw in chapter 1, working hours have shown very little decline since. There is really no evidence at all that this act—the first national legislation to regulate hours for a majority of workers in the United States—accelerated the long-term rate of decline in the national average of hours worked. It may, however, have had some medium-term impact. In an interesting study, H. G. Lewis compared the decline of hours of work in the United States in different industries in the years 1929 to 1942 (i.e., from the last year of prosperity to a year subsequent to the passage of the Fair Labor Standards Act). He concluded that the decline of hours in covered industries in this period was greater than could be expected on the basis of the long-term trend in hours.[11]

Studies at the Industry or Firm Level

Attempts have been made to determine whether differences in standard hours have an effect on work times at a microlevel, using cross-section and time-series data for individual industries in the United States, Germany, the United Kingdom, and other countries. Statistical results vary from study to study but generally have been consistent with the view that overtime is higher when the standard workweek is lower, but not so much higher that actual hours are not reduced. Thus these data can be interpreted as indicating that employers avoid some of the impact of a reduction in the hours standard by increasing the amount of overtime, but that they stop short of behaving as some economists predict: they do not actually increase hours of work in their establishments.

Most recently, R. A. Hart has asked whether this failure to observe an increase in hours might be because the industrywide data used in these studies have included both firms that worked overtime and those that did not, and that the theory only applies to the first group.[12] (As we have seen, the theory predicts opposite results for firms not on overtime.) Hart reported on a study by him and Nicholas Wilson, which addressed this problem by breaking down a sample of fifty-two British metalworking firms into two groups: forty-three that did work overtime and nine that did not.[13]

But even when they excluded firms that did not work overtime, they found no support for the theory that a reduction in standard hours increases hours of work. (In fact, actual hours declined by 80 percent of the reduction in standard hours for firms scheduling overtime.) This is of course a very small sample, and it will be interesting to see whether the same result is obtained in large-scale studies.

RELEVANCE OF INDUSTRY STUDIES FOR NATIONAL POLICY

A more serious specification problem of these industry studies for our purpose is that they do not measure before-and-after results of a national policy of hours reduction. Much of the variation in standard hours in these data occurs because of differences in union contracts—between industries in a cross-section or over time. Most of the remainder can be accounted for by differences in employer policy or state regulation. Hence, much of the variation is endogenous, due to differences in the preferences of the work force or to differences in the technical and institutional characteristics of industries. For example, in a cross-sectional analysis of industries, one might find that some have a shorter standard workweek because they employ a largely female work force, while others have a shorter week because of difficult working conditions in their establishments. And in a study of changes over time in an industry, an increased demand for leisure by the work force may account for a decline in the standard workweek. True, the more sophisticated of these studies do try to account for this endogenous variation (for example, by holding constant the proportion of women employed in an industry), but this effort can be only partially successful—many unmeasured factors remain.

One would expect that such endogenous variations in the standard workweek would be accompanied by variations in the same direction in actual hours, with a minimal effort by employers to offset them by increasing overtime. Profit-maximizing employers operating without intervention by a union or by the state have varied hours in accordance with differences in the nature of the work or in the composition or preferences of their work forces. Of course, cross-sectional and time-series variations in standard hours can also reflect a desire by unions, employers, and others to share work opportunities. But it is difficult to say how important this factor is in the data used for these statistical estimations.

It is very likely, then, that the overtime offset (i.e., the extent to which increases in overtime offset decline in the standard workweek) observed in these industry studies seriously underestimates the offset that would occur if hours were reduced by national legislation. Work sharing could then be a completely exogenous event, not associated with changes in leisure demanded by employees, or in the nature of work, or in the composition of the work force. Employees and employers alike would then have a stronger inducement to offset the change in the standard workweek by increased overtime working.

Increased Moonlighting and Labor Force Participation

The work-sharing goal of laws regulating maximum hours can also be thwarted by a substantial increase in the proportion of those taking second jobs. It is difficult to predict the likely moonlighting response. However, there is some consensus that moonlighting became more important after the workweek was reduced from the forty-eight-to-fifty-one-hour range in the 1920s and 1930s to the forty-hour standard of the post–World War II period. And it is likely that a major new reduction in the legal workweek would yield another significant increase in moonlighting, for two reasons. One, reducing hours at principal jobs reduces family incomes and is expected to lead to more labor supply on that account; two, shorter schedules make it easier for individuals to work two full-time jobs (or at least a full-time and a part-time job).[14] For the same reasons, a shorter workweek is expected to increase the number of job seekers, including housewives wanting to return to the labor market and students and retirees looking for extra income. Again, there is a lack of data on the expected size of this reaction, although most observers predict that it would be significant.

An increase in the number of job seekers does not negate the job creation goal of work-sharing legislation, but it does make it less likely that the program would reduce the number of unemployed.

Summary and Conclusions

The effect of a mandated reduction in the workweek from forty to, say, thirty-five or thirty hours a week is likely to be a smaller reduction in actual work time. Some employees are not covered by the Fair Labor Standards Act, and others work for employers who evade the law. Legal avoidance is also possible when employers can lower real hourly wage rates or raise fringe benefits relative to earnings. Moreover, where wages and fringe benefits are fixed, economic theory predicts that a reduction in the standard workweek is likely to yield longer schedules for those already working overtime. As a result of these several factors, overtime is likely to be sharply higher, and moonlighting is likely to increase.

Many of these problems could be resolved through forceful government action: exemptions could be eliminated and evasion rigorously prosecuted.

In addition, the penalty overtime rate could be raised to double time, or mandatory overtime could be banned. These two measures are discussed in an important study of work time reduction by Ronald Ehrenberg and Paul Schumann, who derive some cautious estimates of their likely effect.[15]

More aggressive action could also be taken: triple time could be demanded; or overtime could be banned altogether.[16] Moonlighting could also be discouraged or banned. These actions would very likely yield a substantial reduction in work time, though at significant economic and social cost. They would obviously require a broad social commitment, and it is not clear whether this level of commitment would ever be given to a policy of reducing unemployment through work sharing.[17]

CHAPTER SIX

The Firm's Economic Efficiency

EVEN if the firm is induced by national work-sharing legislation to reduce hours per employee, it is by no means certain that this will increase the number of people employed. The firm may respond by reducing its output. Or it may endeavor to maintain production without adding new employees, or by adding only a few. This chapter focuses on one important element in the puzzle: the effect of hours reduction on the number of employee hours required per unit of output. Several factors are discussed here, including the effects of a mandated hours reduction on labor hoarding; employee effort per hour; fixed personnel requirements (setup costs, coordination and communication costs, and training costs); and capital utilization effects. The theoretical expectations of these effects are presented first, and then some empirical evidence is discussed.

The firm may also react in more complex ways to thwart the purpose of the legislation. For example, it may find that when hours are lower, labor productivity is reduced, and the resulting increase in costs may induce it to cut output and employment. A discussion of these reactions is deferred until chapter 8.

Labor Hoarding

The term *labor hoarding* in this context refers to the tendency of employers to maintain higher employment than is needed for current output during periods of slack demand. This practice has been described by institutionalist labor economists and by industrial relations specialists for many years, and more recently econometric estimates have been obtained that are consistent with the hypothesis that widespread labor hoarding is practiced during recessions in the United States as well as in Europe.[1]

A direct estimate of the extent of labor hoarding has been computed by Jon Fay and James Medoff on the basis of questionnaires submitted to managers in a number of U.S. manufacturing facilities. According to the authors, "during its most recent trough quarter the typical plant that had a downturn paid for about 8% more blue-collar labor hours than were technologically necessary to meet that quarter's regular production and operations requirements. About half of this labor could be justified by the value of other work (such as additional maintenance, cleaning, training, and so on) that was completed during the trough quarter."[2]

A number of explanations have been given for labor hoarding. In Europe, the high dismissal costs typically imposed provide an obvious explanation. In the United States, dismissal costs are generally much lower (even if the effect of layoffs on future unemployment insurance premiums are taken into account), but union contracts often place other limits on layoffs or on the reassignment of labor during a recession. In addition, the fear of losing employees who have been screened and trained and who will be needed when conditions improve; the desire to maintain a reputation as a good employer (and hence the future ability to obtain qualified employees at a competitive wage); the need to maintain the morale of the work force; and more altruistic concerns can also induce employers to minimize layoffs.[3]

If the firm is hoarding labor during a period of slack demand, and a work time reduction is then imposed upon it, the firm may respond by drawing down this reserve. If the reserve is large enough and the reduction in hours sufficiently modest, the firm can even maintain ouput without any new hires.[4] Moreover, if the work time reduction is widespread in the industry or in the economy, the firm need not fear that its reduced labor hoarding will lead to a higher quit rate or to a reputation as a bad employer.

The significance of labor hoarding will depend upon the length of the run considered: it is important in the short run—in the downward swing of the cycle—but is expected to diminish in the longer run, and eventually to disappear. If low demand persists and appears to the firm as permanent, its motivation for maintaining a reserve of labor for future expansion is obviously reduced. At the same time, the excess work force will be gradually reduced through quits, retirements, and the like, without recourse to layoffs. Hence, labor hoarding is apt to be of only moderate importance in the longer run. Insofar as it is significant, it will constitute a partial offset to the downward effect of hours reduction on the firm's effective labor input.

Worker Effort per Hour

A reduction in work time may also yield an increase in the amount of effort the employee puts in during each hour of work, and this can moderate or even eliminate the effect on effective labor input. The importance of this factor is likely to depend upon the form that the reduction in work time takes—a shorter workday, workweek, or work year. Most studies of the relation between work time and effective worker effort consider variations in the workday. We have seen, though, that much of the reduction in work time in the period since World War II has taken the form of increases in annual vacations and holidays, and relatively little is known about the relation between these holidays and worker effort in the remainder of the year. Reduction of the workweek by reducing the number of workdays (by introducing a four-day, eight-hour-day, week) would provide an interesting case, intermediate between reduction in the workday and reduction in the work year through more vacation time. Some observers believe that it would yield a reduction in worker effort, while others are concerned about the effects of strenuous long weekends on work force productivity. But if the reduction did take the form of a cut in the workday, a case can be made for expecting at least some increase in hourly effort. Moreover, this gain (unlike that resulting from a reduction in labor hoarding) may be long lasting.

The issue of effort per hour is controversial and poses a number of unresolved questions. Often, writers on hours reduction simply assume some conventional size for this effect—for example, that it is sufficient to offset one-third of hours reduction (popular among European trades unionists). More serious efforts to resolve this issue have sometimes endeavored to determine the maximum productivity gain that would be physically possible if hours were reduced. We will also ask a somewhat different question: what actually will be the effect on effort if work time is reduced?

Potential Effects

Lack of physical fatigue is the reason most frequently given for expecting worker effort per hour to increase when hours of work are cut. The argument can be stated either simply, in terms of pieces of work produced per hour by the employee, or in a more sophisticated form, taking into account effects on quality of product, employee accident rates, damage to machinery, and the like. But using any of these measures, most observers believe that if hours of work are extended, total effective daily effort will increase at a diminishing rate, and that if hours are sufficiently extended, the worker's daily contribution will actually fall.

In fact, some economists believe that the very long hours of work scheduled in the textile and other industries a century and a half ago were actually in excess of the output-maximizing level.[5] There is a broader consensus that, as daily hours were decreased in subsequent decades (from, say, twelve to eight per day), the resulting decline in effective labor input was less than in proportion to the reduction in hours. (For example, it can be plausibly argued that the speedups of the Henry Ford era would not have been possible if the workday had remained at ten or twelve hours.)

There is much less agreement, though, on the effect of a reduction in work time below the eight-hour level, since many believe that the reduction in fatigue and hence the potential increase in hourly effort will be less.[6] In some work situations, hours are now sufficiently short that fatigue is no longer a significant problem. (Indeed, it has been argued that further cuts will result in more time spent in strenuous leisure activities, with less energy left for the job.[7]) In other, more demanding, work situations a reduction in fatigue could yield some additional gains if work time were reduced. A further complication is that individual workers vary widely in their ability to supply effort: some manage to complete a given work assignment only by making a maximal effort, while others do it with ease. Shorter hours may then improve the productivity of the first type of worker but not the second.

The theoretical and scientific results of ergonomic research shed some light on the relation between shorter hours and worker performance.[8] This research confirms the view that the effects of fatigue depend upon the type of work, the characteristics of the worker, and other circumstances. But its findings are consistent with the view that shorter hours permit higher effort per hour. For many workers and for many types of work, this continues to be true as the work period is reduced below the eight-hour level.

One must use caution, though, in applying such results in a discussion of the work-sharing question. Studies of the effects of work schedules on fatigue and output are often carried out in laboratory or other controlled conditions, limiting their value in dealing with the industrial relations questions posed by work-sharing policy. They are perhaps most useful in telling us how people can perform when they are making a maximum effort to meet the demands of their jobs. Indeed, such research is often used to predict the reaction of soldiers under conditions of maximum stress.

Physical constraints may also have been of paramount concern when workers lived at subsistence levels and had relatively little choice but to work near their physical capacity level in order to survive (although the history of industrialization in Europe and America is filled with examples of the resistance of workers to factory discipline, despite their wretchedly poor living conditions). Even today, such constraints apply when the firm can demand maximum effort from its workers. (For example, it has been reported that in jobs where the employer requires an unusually large amount of physical energy, part-time employees are significantly more productive.) However, the condition of the *average* industrial or service sector worker in the United States today is hardly comparable to that of the soldier in combat or a proletarian at the edge of starvation—workers may or may not exert 100 percent of their potential effort on the job.

Such agnosticism on worker effort is based in part on empirical observation: many writers have noted instances of American and European employees working at low intensity. Moreover, the time-budget data for Americans discussed in the appendix to chapter 1 indicate that about forty-five minutes a day is taken in breaks. It is not clear whether this over- or underestimates the amount of slack in the day's effort. On the one hand, many breaks are productive in nature. On the other hand, time spent on a task is just one measure of work effort: the intensity of effort may be less than the employee's full potential, and these time-budget data do not measure this. Hence, a scientific study of the effects of fatigue— while valuable in predicting the potential gains from hours reduction—is of only limited assistance in forecasting the effect of shorter hours on worker effort. For this purpose, we will turn from the question of what workers *could do* with a shorter workday to a discussion of what they are *likely to do.*

LIKELY EFFECTS

Neoclassical Economic Theory. The neoclassical economic theory of shirking provides some basis for prediction. The theory's analysis begins by assuming that a worker's utility is determined by the effort put in each hour, the length of the workday, and the wages received. In a very simple model of the workplace, employees receive an hourly wage in proportion to their productive effort (a very rough approximation to this situation is found in some piece-rate systems of compensation). Employees then face a trade-off between working less per hour and earning less and working more per hour and earning more.

More sophisticated theories of worker effort—or of shirking—have been advanced by economists in the last ten years.[9] These theories take into account that most employees are paid by the hour rather than by the piece: their choice may be between low effort, which may result in dismissal, and high effort, which may reduce the probability of dismissal and may increase the likelihood of promotion.

Some of these theories also assume that the employer has difficulty in determining who is shirking, in the sense of supplying less than potential effort. The employer either cannot monitor the individual's contribution or cannot ascertain the individual's ability to perform. The latter consideration becomes important when individuals in the labor pool from which the employer draws vary in ability. In this situation, those performing above some minimum standard may still be shirking, in that they are not giving 100 percent of their effort.

Various schemes have been devised that rational employers might use to deal with the shirking problem, including: expending more resources on supervision to acquire information on individual performance and ability; paying a wage greater than the market wage (or at least a wage that makes the job more attractive than a spell of unemployment) and then relying on the employee's fear of being dismissed for shirking; providing an upward trajectory of wages with seniority, with a pension at the end of the working life, for those who are not caught shirking and therefore dismissed; or offering promotions to those with good production records. In the neoclassical model, these management strategies cause employees to balance their desire to shirk against their desire to keep their jobs and hence to maintain present and future income. As in the simple payment-by-the-piece case, the employee must choose between more income and less effort.

Neoclassical theory generally predicts that a reduction in scheduled hours will be accompanied by an increase in effort per hour (as long as the employer raises hourly compensation as effort is increased). This emerges most clearly in the simple model, where employees are paid by the piece and have complete freedom in determining the work pace. A reduction in hours also reduces income and hence raises the marginal utility of income to them (by the usual assumption that the marginal utility of income increases as there is less of it). The hours reduction probably also decreases the marginal disutility of effort per hour. An increase in the marginal utility of income accompanied by a likely decrease in the marginal disutility of effort per hour will, in this neoclassical framework, predict that workers will be willing to trade more effort per hour to obtain income. The outcome is not so obvious in a complicated model of shirking behavior. However, if income and daily effort are reduced by a work-sharing rule, one would predict that, ceteris paribus, increased hourly effort could be obtained.[10]

Alternative Theories. However, some caution must be exercised in using neoclassical conclusions for policy purposes. A variety of competing theories address the motivation of workers and work groups, and they do not offer unambiguous resolutions of the effect of hours reduction.

In the first place, effort in a modern employment setting is not a unidimensional index of physical labor but rather a complex set of employee behaviors that will serve to increase the employer's profits—including, for example, the effort of the employee to be cooperative, patient, steady, responsible, personable, and assertive. Moreover, individuals vary widely in their willingness or ability to offer these behaviors. They cannot be changed at will. Even where an improvement is possible for an individual, it may require a lengthy learning period. For example, there is a large literature on how those new to factory or office discipline (former farmers, students, members of an "underclass," to name but a few) take years to learn to supply a different type of effort, often at considerable personal and social cost. Hence, one might expect only a modest increase in some types of effort per hour as hours are reduced, at least in the short run. (For example, as their hours are reduced, one might predict a smaller gain in the persuasive powers of sales personnel than in the hourly effort of furniture movers.)

Prediction of the effort-hours relation becomes still more complex when one tries to take into account the various psychological and managerial approaches to increasing effort. These typically reject the assumption of a static utility function (in which workers seek to minimize their effort) in favor of an approach in which management can induce workers to have a positive attitude toward their effort by paying attention to their needs for achievement and recognition, by giving them appropriate material rewards, and by using other psychologically oriented techniques.[11] Movement to a seven- or six-hour day would undoubtedly see the birth of new managerial techniques, designed to exploit the possibilities for increasing employees' motivation to supply more effort per hour, but such innovations are of course not readily forecastable.

Perhaps the most telling critique of a simple neoclassical view is offered by those who support a group conflict theory of the determination of worker effort. One finds in the writings of Marxians, socialists, and other critics of the industrial order a strong tradition of analysis of worker effort in terms of employer attempts to maintain or increase work norms and of employee resistance to this pressure. Indeed, some radicals have considered this ongoing conflict to be the essence of the contemporary class struggle.[12]

A recent article by Samuel Bowles endeavored to bridge the gap between the neoclassical analysis of shirking and a Marxian, or at least a radical, perspective.[13] Bowles argued that the contractual arrangements between employers and employees are "incomplete," in that they detail wages, fringe benefits, and hours of work, but do not specify the amount of work that the employee will perform in each hour. The required level of effort is determined through struggle.

A related literature has focused attention on how organizational and technological changes have helped employers impose a more stringent work discipline and hence increase effort.[14] Such changes are sometimes seen (especially by radical analysts) as resulting from employer efforts to gain control of workers. Other writers tend to regard them as exogenously determined by technical progress. But it is difficult to dispute the influence of technology on worker effort. For example, the introduction of mass production technologies in industry is said to have given management greater control of blue collar workers. New technologies replaced traditional crafts and skills, which were partly controlled by employees, with a system that permitted employers to define jobs and skills and to set work norms. The famous speedups in the automobile industry in the preunion era were then possible. A more recent example is the expanded use of computers, which permit even greater employer control (for example, by counting keystrokes of typists and measuring the length of conversations of telephone operators).

Insofar as workers' effort is determined by group struggle—including management trying to gain control over workers by means of technical and organizational innovations and workers resisting speedups—an element of indeterminacy is introduced. At the very least, we must say that the neoclassical prediction will be mediated by the political and industrial relations environment in which hours reduction takes place.

This obviously makes a forecast of the effect of hours reduction more difficult. If effort per hour is determined by social, political, industrial relations, psychological, cultural, and other factors, as well as by the physical effects of fatigue, then even the most cleverly designed empirical efforts to determine the relation between hours and daily effort is unlikely to yield generalizable results: the hours-effort relation observed in one time, place, or industrial sector need not prevail in another, but will instead be highly dependent upon the circumstances in which the reduction takes place. And even when those circumstances are fairly well known, it will be difficult to predict the outcome unless the *expectations* of employers and employees about future behavior are also specified.

Consider a hypothetical example in which workers are offered a shorter workweek without any reduction in pay on the condition that they maintain output. They are currently supplying much less than 100 percent of their effort. It might appear reasonable to predict that they will respond to the offer with a sharp increase in effort per hour. However, this prediction may be incorrect. If the employees believe that the firm is making the offer simply to determine the extent to which they can be speeded up—that is, to reveal their true abilities, their devices for informally restricting output, and other facts concealed from management—and that the firm intends to raise hours again once it has acquired this knowledge, they will be wise to reject the offer and to affect ignorance of any means of increasing their productivity.

In summary, there are good reasons to expect an increase in employee effort if work time is reduced as a work-sharing device during a period of high unemployment, but the extent of the increase (if any) must depend on the scenario in which hours are cut.[15]

Fixed Personnel Costs

Another factor that influences how a reduction in hours of work affects the economic efficiency of the firm is the real costs (in the sense of necessary time taken away from productive work) that rise with the number of workers, rather than with the total number of hours worked. They include training costs, communication and coordination costs, and setup costs. All of these fixed cost factors tend to reduce labor input per hour as hours are reduced, an effect opposite to that of labor hoarding and changes in employees' hourly effort.

In most jobs, a period of time is required for the new worker to reach the same level of competence as more senior employees. This period generally extends well beyond any formal training period but still should be thought of as training time. Other time costs of the training process include the diversion of effort by more senior workers in order to help the new employee. These costs must be considered when discussing the impact of hours reduction on effective labor input. If total hours of work per employee are reduced, and training time per employee is not, then obviously hours of work per employee spent in production must be reduced disproportionately. Hence, effective labor input per hour of work paid for declines.

A similar argument applies to daily setup costs. In many shop situations, a worker will spend a half hour or more getting his machinery and tools ready for the day's work. A reduction in the workday will then yield a more than proportionate reduction in effective work time. Of course, if the work time reduction takes the form of more days off per week or year, this problem does not arise. In addition, coordination of and communication among workers must be organized by management. If work sharing obtains its desired result of inducing the employer to hire more employees to do the same amount of work, then the required coordination and communications linkages are increased, in at least the same proportion, generally imposing higher costs on management.

However, most of these arguments on fixed costs apply better to the case of a long-run reduction in hours of work than to a short-term reduction undertaken in response to a temporary failure in demand. In a recession, few if any new employees are hired. In fact, employers have an interest in maintaining intact their human capital, and a spread-the-work measure may play a positive role here, by averting layoffs of trained personnel. True, the value of this policy to any one firm depends in part on whether other firms also reduce work time. If they do not, its best-trained workers may resent the loss in purchasing power consequent upon a reduction in hours, and may quit; and these quits may be more costly to the firm than the loss of low-seniority workers through layoffs. On the other hand, if the work time reduction is general, incentive to quit is reduced. A similar argument applies to communications and coordination costs. A smaller labor force could reduce these costs, but this will require a basic reorganization of management staff and bookkeeping procedures. It may also require a reduction in the white collar work force. All this takes time. Moreover, such changes also require an initial investment of management resources and so will not be undertaken if the reduction in output is regarded as temporary. Hence, this argument would be important only in the longer run.

Thus, these fixed cost factors are not likely to constitute a significant offset to the fatigue and labor hoarding effects in the short run but will become more important as the run becomes longer. Recall also that the labor hoarding effect is expected to diminish with time. Hence, if a medium-run reduction in hours were instituted, lasting at least several years, the negative long-term effects on labor utilization might in time come to dominate any positive initial short-term effects on effective labor input per hour.

Capital Utilization

The foregoing argument is reinforced when one considers the impact of hours reduction on the efficiency with which capital is utilized. If hours are *not* reduced when demand is slack, employers can sometimes improve efficiency by closing down older, inefficient, labor-intensive plants and concentrating production in more efficient production lines or facilities. These efforts will be less effective if employers reduce hours per employee rather than lay off employees. Then production is maintained even in the less-efficient, labor-intensive facilities: workers on production lines of different vintages working in different plants simply reduce their hours of work. Hence, more labor hours are needed to maintain production, on this argument, if hours reduction is substituted for employment reduction.[16]

It has been objected that this argument does not apply in establishments where multiple shifts are worked. If an employment reduction takes the form of canceling second or third shifts, a reduction in capital utilization takes place parallelling that seen when hours per worker are reduced: the daily hours of operation of machinery are reduced. Multiple shifts are, of course, fairly common in the traditional industrial core of the economy: manufacturing and mining. But shifts of overlapping part- and full-time employees are also used in the retail trade and service sectors, where they enable establishments to extend hours of operation. Hence, this objection has some empirical validity. (Compare the discussion in chapter 10.)

But despite this exception, many observers believe that substituting reductions in hours for reductions in employees has deleterious effects on capital utilization, and hence requires a greater total number of hours per unit of output. This effect is likely to be greater in the medium run than in the very short run: at least some time is required for inefficient plants and firms to stop production and output to be concentrated in more modern, capital-intensive establishments. But in the evaluation of a medium-term policy, the opportunity cost to productive efficiency of not making these adjustments is expected to be significant.

Summary and Empirical Evidence

Some short-term reduction in the amount of labor used per unit of output is likely if working hours are reduced. Labor hoarding is expected to be less and, in a favorable industrial relations climate, workers may be induced to supply more effort per hour. But as the short run is extended into the medium run, productivity gains of hours reduction are likely to be less and may eventually turn into losses. A policy of hours reduction in place of layoffs means that the firm must forgo some advantages it might otherwise obtain. These include closing inefficient plants and concentrating production in modern facilities as well as streamlining managerial structures to take advantage of the lower communications and coordinations costs of a smaller work force. And when new hires must eventually be made, a larger work force means a greater investment in hiring, screening, and training costs. In the longer run, then, work time reduction could well mean higher labor input requirements per unit of output. (See also the discussion of long-term effects in chapter 12.)

This analysis implies that if employers were to maintain output in the face of a mandated reduction in hours per worker, then in the short run a less-than-proportionate increase in employment (or reduction in layoffs) will be required, but that in the somewhat longer run a more-than-proportionate increase in employment may be needed.

It is not surprising that efforts to obtain a *definitive* empirical estimate of the substitution possibilities between hours per employee and number of employees in producing output have been unsatisfactory. There are a number of determinants of this relation: some predict an increase in labor required per unit of output as hours are reduced, and some a decrease. Moreover, as the period in which hours are reduced is extended from the short run to the longer run, the relative importance and, in some cases, the sign of these influences are predicted to change. Further, the relation is expected to depend upon the industrial relations climate in which hours reduction is introduced. Under these circumstances, the effort to find a definitive, simple relation may be a search for a will-o'-the-wisp.

Much of the empirical literature, however, focuses not on these more fundamental issues but rather on the advantages and disadvantages of various methods of estimation. For example, one of the simplest ways to calculate the relation between hours of work and effort is to observe how work effort varies as employees near the end of the workday. Typically, some falloff is observed in the last hour. However, this is a very crude method, and economic theory suggests that these variations are not good predictors of the effects of reduced work time. A pioneering paper by two economists, Frank Stafford and Malcolm B. Cohen, pointed out that if workers wished to maximize their daily work output, they should deliberately vary its intensity.[17] The authors suggest that a plausible strategy would be to get off to a slow start after lunch in order to reserve some energy for the end of the day, when their work would otherwise be seriously flawed. An implication of their model is that one cannot use observed fluctuations in output over the hours of the day as a guide to hourly output variations that would be found if hours were reduced: the observed falloff would underestimate the effect of fatigue. Similarly, the frequently observed weekly pattern of lower output on *both* Mondays and Fridays may be explained by sociological or psychological factors but does not help us to predict the effect of a shorter workweek.

Another simple way to assess the effect of hours reduction is to survey employers and obtain their subjective evaluation. Economists have a tradition of preferring objective evidence over such managerial evaluations. But the latter do have the great advantage that they have been carried out either before or after state- or union-mandated reductions in hours. These surveys have found that many employers in France and Germany react by speeding up workers, reducing dead time (especially through more efficient scheduling of labor, machinery, and materials), and in other ways increasing labor productivity.[18] Trade unions are also reported, in some instances, to make concessions on work rules in order to obtain shorter hours.[19]

A third method is to observe output in one or more plants as hours of work change. Unfortunately, this method does not allow one to hold factors other than hours reduction constant. For example, the U.S. Department of Labor studies of U.S. factories during World War II were long regarded as providing the best evidence of the negative effects on productivity of fatigue when hours are very long. But Irving Leveson subsequently showed that these measurements were taken as hours were *reduced* in war plants from quite high levels (often sixty or more per week) toward the forty-hour standard.[20] This period of hours reduction coincided with a decline in wartime demand and an easing of the wartime labor shortage, which permitted firms to eliminate less-efficient employees. Hence, Leveson argues, the production data reflect more than the effect of hours reduction.[21]

A fourth method of ascertaining the relative importance of hours and employment is to estimate output as a function of these variables and other standardizing variables, using data broken down to at least the industry level. The data base may be a cross-section of industries, a time series, or a pooled time series and cross-section (i.e., a number of industries, each observed over a period of years).

The econometric estimates obtained in this way have not been satisfactory.[22] In the first place, they range widely: some show output to be more sensitive to hours fluctuations than to employment fluctuations, some indicate the reverse, and still others show hours and employment to have roughly equal influences on output. In other words, the results would be consistent with the view that a reduction in hours would require a less-than-proportional, an equal, or a greater-than-proportional increase in number of employees to maintain output.

Moreover, there are serious specification problems in these estimations. Those that are based on time series are heavily influenced by movements over the business cycle, and this introduces measurement difficulties. As demand for an industry's products turns down, less labor is required, but the typical initial reaction of employers is to postpone layoffs: they instead reduce hours and hoard labor. Partly because of labor hoarding, labor productivity often declines as the economy goes into a recession.[23] Hence, one would expect to see a correlation between reduced hours and reduced output per hour. But this correlation should not be interpreted to mean that a reduction in hours *causes* a reduction in the productivity of labor. On the contrary, hours reduction provides an alternative to even more hoarding and so presumably reduces it. In that sense, hours reduction increases labor productivity.

On the other hand, Michael White points out that a spuriously positive relation may be observed between productivity gains and hours reduction when exogenous improvements in productivity in a plant induce management to reduce working hours.[24] For example, a firm may want to introduce a new, productivity-enhancing technology while minimizing the number of layoffs, and it initiates a work-sharing policy for this purpose. These examples illustrate the difficulty of using time-series data to make inferences about the effect of hours reduction on production per hour.

In a sense, cross-sectional estimates based on observations of different industries are still more unsatisfactory. Some of the interindustry variation represents short-term factors, such as those observed over the cycle. For example, in a given year the computer and robotics industry may expand rapidly while the textile industry enters a depression and automobile production stagnates. The measurement problems here are similar to those observed for the time-series data discussed above.

Cross-sectional variations also reflect long-term, equilibrium differences among industries: some have longer schedules on a more or less permanent basis. However, a special type of measurement problem arises here. In a cross-sectional analysis, the value added per worker is used as a measure of the worker's output. But value is calculated by multiplying the price of the good or service by the quantity; and under competitive conditions, price differences will, in equilibrium, reflect differences in costs, such as those due to industry differences in hourly wage rates. Hence, an interindustry difference in productivity may actually reflect a difference in hourly wages. This has implications for measuring the relation between hours and productivity. If workers do not want to work long hours and if they require higher hourly wages (or the payment of an overtime premium) to do so, one will see a correlation between wages and hours. But if wage differences are reflected in measured productivity differences, then a spuriously positive correlation is generated between hours and productivity.

Finally, long-term, equilibrium variations in work times are not expected to have the same relation to hourly effort that one might see if hours were reduced as part of a work-sharing effort. For example, with work sharing, the employed worker has more leisure and less income than he or she would have in a free-market outcome, and this is expected to induce the worker to supply more effort per hour in order to earn more income. But no such effect is expected when one compares industries with relatively short hours (say, in the thirty-five-to-thirty-nine-hour-a-week range) with industries with longer hours. Industries with shorter hours can recruit workers who prefer shorter hours and somewhat lower weekly wages. (In fact, hourly as well as weekly wages are often lower in these industries.) For example, these industries often employ a high percentage of women, whose outside responsibilities prevent them from working longer hours. A more positive effect on hourly productivity may result when shorter hours are imposed on all workers, regardless of their preferences.[25]

The empirical evidence on the effects of hours reduction on the need to hire more labor to maintain output is weak. Perhaps the most one can do is not reject the hypothesis that a reduction in hours would require a less than proportionate increase in employment, if production were to be maintained.

CHAPTER SEVEN

Effects on Wages

Money Wages

THE EFFECTS of a work-sharing policy will depend in large measure on whether hours reduction is accompanied by an increase in hourly compensation. If hourly wages are increased, the income loss of those workers whose hours are reduced and who keep their jobs is less. However, an increase in money wages is likely to have a negative effect on employment and hence to have a contrary effect on work-sharing policy. (This employment effect is explored in chapters 8 and 9.[1])

There is virtual unanimity that hours reduction is likely to lead to some increase in hourly wages. Trade unions, which have forcefully advocated work time reduction, have typically made this demand. Governments sympathetic to work time reduction have also often been supportive of compensating wage increases. For example, Jean Pierre Jallade reported that when hours of work were reduced by law in France in 1982, the confederations of French unions and employers tried to work out a compromise on the issue of pay and were making some progress.[2] However, the French socialist government intervened in the midst of these negotiations and ruled that full compensation must be paid the workers. There are numerous other recent examples of work time reduction being accompanied by at least partial compensation in wages, with or without government intervention, including agreements in the 1980s in West Germany and in Great Britain to reduce hours below the forty-per-week standard.

Of course, it is often difficult in practice to determine whether a given wage increase is due to an hours reduction or would have occurred in any event. If the hours reduction is modest, a relatively small wage increase will compensate for it. And if the work time reduction is granted at contract renewal time—when a wage increase would be expected in any event—it is sometimes difficult to determine whether the wage rise is larger as a result of the hours reduction. However, the widespread belief that wage increases under these circumstances are in fact larger than normal and the common-sense argument that this is a reasonable expectation are both supported by economic theory. Economists have used two basic models to analyze the effect of hours reduction on wages. In the first, the employer sets the wage. In the second, the union does.[3]

EMPLOYERS AND WAGE SETTING

In the employer wage-setting model, the firm is interested in minimizing its unit labor costs.[4] This of course encourages the firm to seek lower wages. It does not, however, provide an incentive for it to minimize the hourly wage, since the firm is also assumed to have an interest in reducing the quit rate of its employees (in part because of the investment it has made in hiring, screening, and training). The quit rate is assumed to be a negative function of the wage the firm pays relative to the market wage. Hence, the rational employer will set a wage that strikes a balance between gain from a lower wage bill and gain from a lower quit rate.

However, all firms cannot be paying a greater than market wage—their average wage determines the market wage. The equilibrating mechanism here for equating wage offers to the market wage is the unemployment rate. The quit rate is assumed to be a negative function of the unemployment rate as well as of the wage rate. Hence, a sufficiently high national unemployment rate enables the average firm to keep its quit rate down to a satisfactory level without paying a high wage: that is, the firm will reduce its wage level to that of the market. When hours reduction is introduced into this model, its initial effect is to reduce unemployment and so induce firms to increase wages, to prevent their quit rates from rising. Moreover, a reduction in hours yields an increase in the relative importance of training and other fixed costs (since these must now be balanced against fewer hours of actual work), giving further incentives to firms to raise wages in order to discourage quits.

One can also speculate that a weekly wage decline of a substantial amount would itself yield an increase in the quit rate, giving firms an additional incentive to raise wages. For some employees, the reduction in their weekly wage income will provide the spur to look elsewhere, even though wages incomes elsewhere will have been reduced as well. Because of inertia or because of nonfinancial advantages of their present employment, workers often stay in jobs that pay them less than they could earn elsewhere. However, a sudden sharp reduction in their pay packets may provide the needed incentive to search for more remunerative employment.[5]

One could go beyond these models and find other reasons for employers to raise wages after hours are cut. Without the increase, morale would sink as employees found their living standard reduced. In some circumstances, this would not be important enough to move the firm to raise its labor costs by a wage increase, but there are recorded instances when employers have behaved this way.[6]

Unions and Wage Setting

Other economists have assumed that trade unions determine wages, then have asked whether a reduction in hours would tend to incline them toward raising wages.[7] In most of these efforts, the well-known monopoly union model is employed, in which the union has a monopoly in the industry or even in the economy, but employers are divided and hence act in competition with each other. This imbalance permits the union to set wages. This situation is said to characterize industrial relations in several European countries. Although it prevails in the United States only where a strong union has organized an industry dominated by relatively small firms, the usefulness of the model extends beyond these limited applications.[8] If one knows the unions' preference function—the conditions it would impose if it had the monopoly power to do so—one has a basis for understanding outcomes where the result depends upon bargaining between employers and unions (obviously the more common situation among American workers who are unionized).

The union is assumed here to be concerned about income and leisure (i.e., it is assumed to maximize a utility function whose arguments are income and leisure). Income is generally specified as the wage for the employed and as unemployment benefits for the unemployed. Leisure is time not spent working. The union's problem is that it faces a trade-off: as it raises wages, employers reduce the number of jobs. (Unions do not bargain over or otherwise control the employment decisions of employers.) Hence, a wage hike raises the income of those who keep their jobs but moves some others into the ranks of the unemployed, where their income is less though their leisure is much increased (perhaps to an undesirable level). In these models, the union chooses a wage rate that balances off the change in the well-being of the job keepers to that of the job losers. (In a growing industry, it may also consider the well-being of potential new entrants, or job gainers.[9])

Typically, the effect of an exogenously determined reduction in hours in this model is to increase the wage rate set by the union. There are several reasons for this. First, the reduction in wage income of the employed increases the weight they give to obtaining higher wages—to partially offset income loss.[10] Second, if the decline in hours does reduce unemployment among members, this reduces the pressure on the union to consider unemployment effects when setting the wage. Another possible effect occurs if the greater leisure enjoyed by the employed increases the utility of money over leisure (because of the greater leisure time opportunities for spending money) and so raises their wage demands. Other effects of hours reduction include a decrease in the leisure forgone by working and hence the disutility of working relative to being unemployed, which partly offset the fact that income gain from working has also been lowered. The net effect of these several changes may be to induce the union to set a higher hourly wage rate.

Introduction of longer term considerations produces an interesting variation in this model.[11] If the union's policy of raising wages at the expense of declining employment eventually leads to a smaller membership, then those who were laid off in the earlier periods may no longer count in the union's decision making, either as members or in any other way. In that sense, the union may become progressively more biased toward higher wages, accepting a gradually reduced work force. On the other hand, the union may not wish to face a long-term decline in its membership. Moreover, it has been argued that, once the union considers long-term effects, it may begin to take into account the effect of its wage policy on such long-range employer strategies as substituting capital for labor or moving capital out of the industry. This would also help to moderate union pressure for higher wages.[12]

EMPLOYER-UNION WAGE SETTING

In a third model of wage determination, the employer or union monopoly model is replaced by a bilateral monopoly model, in which wages are determined by collective bargaining. A paper by Alison Booth and Fabio Schiantarelli analyzing the effect of an exogenous decline in hours on the bargain over wage rates struck when management and unions are each influenced by the considerations given here (i.e., management wants to reduce labor costs and the union will trade off jobs for higher wage rates) concludes that the result will generally be higher wages.[13]

CONCLUSIONS

Whether the employer, the union, or the bargaining model is used, the conclusion is that an exogenously determined hours reduction will generally be expected to increase wages, because a reduction in unemployment exerts upward pressure on wages. In addition, independent effects of hours reduction tend to increase wages: employers are influenced by the greater relative cost of a quit, while unions are concerned with restoring the purchasing power of their employed members.

While there is consensus on the direction of change in wages, there is, unfortunately, equal consensus that such models do not predict the size of the change. Partial, full, or even more than full, compensation for hours reduction are all possible outcomes in these models.

Fringe Benefits and Related Wage Costs

Compensation costs per hour worked increase when hours are reduced—quite apart from any increase in hourly wages—since some major fringe benefits are fixed per worker, rather than per hour. Perhaps the most important of these is the employer contribution to the employee's health care. Other benefits vary with earnings but only up to a maximum level. For those who earn above that maximum, the fringe benefit is a fixed cost. An example of this type of benefit is the employer contribution to unemployment insurance. These fixed costs are powerful disincentives for the employer considering hours reduction. They are said to be a key factor in the disappointingly low rate of employer participation in short-time compensation schemes in those states that provide that option.

Of course, some fixed fringe benefits might not remain fixed if work time is reduced for a prolonged period. For example, if hours reduction takes the form of a temporary reduction in the workweek—accomplished by reducing overtime and increasing short time—vacation and holiday pay would, for the most part, be unaffected, and hence could be considered as a fixed cost. But once a new, lower *standard* of hours was established, vacation and holiday pay would be reduced. For example, if the standard workweek was cut from forty hours to, say, thirty-five, vacation and holiday pay would undoubtedly be calculated on the basis of the lower earnings obtained on this shorter schedule and would be reduced accordingly. However, a variety of other compensation costs, including those for health care, employee recreation facilities, education programs, and so on, would not be so readily reduced as the standard wage cut and so would function as at least quasi-fixed costs in the context of a medium-term work-sharing policy.

It is often said that a reduction in hours would, by reducing unemployment, lower the unemployment tax rate for the firm. This argument would not apply if, as many advocates of work sharing urge, workers would obtain unemployment benefits when on short time. In any event, this argument applies only to the extent to which hours reduction actually leads to a reduction in unemployment.[14]

CHAPTER EIGHT

The Firm's Employment Decision

THE DISCUSSION of the effects of work time policy on employment has identified several effects. If successful, it will reduce work time per employee, change the number of hours required per unit of output (though the direction of the change is unclear—probably negative in the short run and positive in the long run), and raise labor costs per hour worked. These various impacts will influence employment. In this chapter we consider how such changes will affect employment decisions of the typical firm or industry. In the next chapter, employment effects at the level of the economy are discussed.

Economic Models

In modeling the reaction of the firm to hours reduction, the output of a firm is typically treated as a function of such factors of production as number of employees, hours worked per employee, and capital stock.[1] In the medium-run analysis considered here, capital stock is treated as a constant. Output changes occur only as a function of changes in number of employees or hours per worker. Even with these simplifying assumptions, different microeconomic models yield a wide variety of predicted impacts on the firm's demand for labor. This can be seen by considering just a few basic models.

Two Basic Models

In a very simple model of employment, the firm's output is given exogenously by market conditions, although the firm can vary the number of workers and the number of hours per worker so as to minimize the cost of producing that output. This cost-minimization model is often used in conjunction with a Keynesian macroeconomic model and so has been dubbed the Keynesian microeconomic model for evaluating the effects of hours reduction.[2] If output is fixed, as in this Keynesian model (and the assumption of constant capital stock continues to be employed), a reduction in hours per worker must be offset by a fully compensating change in the number of employees: that is, one that will keep effective labor input constant.

In an alternative model, more in the neoclassical tradition, the firm can choose its level of output and does so to maximize its profits. This implies that it will increase employment up to the point where the additional sales revenue obtained by hiring additional workers equals the additional costs imposed on the firm by their employment.

In this section, we make the simplifying assumptions that the firm is faced with a constant price for its product and constant hourly compensation for its employees. (These assumptions are dropped later in this chapter.) Then, the change in sales revenue obtained by hiring additional employees is equal to the product of the price per unit of output times the amount of the addition to output due to their employment. The cost incurred by additional hires is simply their hourly compensation. The profit-maximizing firm will then increase employment to the point where the wage equals the output price times the increase in output obtained (i.e., where the wage equals the additional sales revenue obtained by hiring a worker).

Alternatively, this profit-maximizing rule can be stated in a more convenient form as the equation of the marginal product of labor to the ratio of output price to wage ($MPL = P/W$). Since we are assuming price and wage to be constant, this rule implies that the marginal product of labor is also constant. **If the wage rate is measured per hour, this means that the marginal product per hour of the labor of an additional employee must be constant, despite a change in the number of hours per worker.** Thus, if the change in hours changes the marginal product per hour of an additional employee, the profit-maximizing employer will change employment until this marginal product is restored to its original level.

For example, if a reduction in hours per employee increases the marginal product per hour of employees, the gain to the employer of hiring an additional worker will then exceed its marginal cost, and the employer will expand employment. But if there are diminishing returns to the number of employees, so that as employment rises the addition to output to be obtained by one more employee falls, the expansion in employment will tend to reduce the marginal product of an hour of work. Profit-maximizing employers will then continue to expand output to the point where this diminishing returns effect has offset the original increase in marginal product, due to shorter hours, and the gain in production from employing still more labor is just offset by the increase in costs.

In summary, the Keynesian model requires that effective labor input or labor services be constant, while the neoclassical model (with the assumptions of constant wages and prices) requires that the marginal product of labor (per hour) be constant.

Four Production Relations Models

In addition to the two-way division between Keynesian and neoclassical models, it is also common in the discussion of the effects of work time reduction to distinguish between several production functions: ways in which labor is assumed to increase output. Four such production relations are considered here.

In the first model, output is a function of capital stock (held constant in the short or medium run) and labor services (L). Labor services here are simply the product of employment (N) and hours per employee (H) (i.e., $L = NH$). **In this model, number of workers and hours per worker are perfect substitutes for each other.** The employer is only concerned about total hours, since there are no diminishing returns from substituting employees for hours per employee, or vice versa. **However, in this model (since capital stock is held constant) output is generally allowed to be subject to diminishing returns from labor services (L): additional labor increases output, but less than proportionately.**

The second model treats labor services very differently. At a given level of hours per worker, capital stock and number of employees interact to produce output. In this interaction, capital stock and number of employees are each subject to diminishing returns if the other factor is held constant. But if capital stock and number of employees are held constant and number of hours per worker increases, output rises in *proportion* to hours—there are no diminishing returns. The rationale for this model is the one-man-one-machine concept of production.[3] In the discussion of capital efficiency in chapter 6 it was pointed out that, while increasing the number of employees and holding constant the number of machines (or capital stock) are expected to yield diminishing returns, **no such diminishing returns are predicted if each employee puts in a longer day: existing stock is simply used for more hours, but there is no increase in the ratio of employees to machines.**

The third model is a variant of the second. **The one-man-one-machine concept is retained, so that output is proportionate to the effective daily labor input of the worker. However, this input is no longer assumed to be proportionate to hours of work.** If fatigue reduces an employee's productivity, input will be subject to diminishing returns as hours increase. If, on the other hand, there are initial daily setup costs, increased daily hours may yield increasing returns.[4]

Finally, the fourth model is the most general. It assumes, like the first, that output is a function of effective labor services and capital stock, subject to diminishing returns in each. However, unlike the first model, hours per worker and number of workers need not be perfect substitutes in producing labor services. **In this more general model, labor services are simply**

a positive function of hours per worker and number of employees. This formulation leaves room for various possibilities of diminishing or increasing returns to each in contributing to labor services (or effective labor input).

EMPLOYMENT EFFECTS OF THE MODELS

Following are the employment effects of hours reduction for the Keynesian and neoclassical versions of each of the four models of production relations.

Production Model 1. The first model assumes perfect substitutability between number of employees and hours per employee. **Then, both the Keynesian and neoclassical models require that a reduction in hours be matched by a proportionate increase in the number of employees.** This keeps constant labor services, or effective labor input used by the firm (since hours of work and number of employees are assumed to be perfect substitutes). In the Keynesian variant, maintenance of labor services at the original level is necessary to keep output constant. In the neoclassical variant, it is necessary to keep constant the marginal contribution of an hour of work by an additional worker. (Since labor services are unchanged as well as capital stock, the marginal product of labor services is kept constant.)

Production Model 2. In this variant of the one-man-one-machine model, output increases in proportion to hours worked. **When one adopts the Keynesian constraint of constant output here, the number of employees must be increased when hours are reduced.** If, as expected, output rises at a decreasing rate as more employees are added, it will be necessary to provide a *more* than proportionate increase in the number of workers in order to maintain output. The neoclassical variant yields a very different result. If output is proportionate to hours per worker, then a reduction in these hours does *not* change the contribution per hour of an additional worker. **Hence, in this case, hours reduction in the neoclassical model provides no incentive to the firm to change the employment level.**

Production Model 3. When this one-man-one-machine model is modified to allow for the effects of fatigue or of fixed daily setup costs to introduce, respectively, decreasing or increasing returns to hours of work per worker, the analysis is more complicated. **The lower the returns to hours of work, the less impact on output results from hours reduction, and, in the Keynesian constant output model, this means a smaller increase in the demand for number of employees.** Hence, where fatigue effects dominate over setup cost effects, the increase in demand for labor is reduced below that predicted by the previous model.[5] In the neoclassical case, the effect is also more complicated when the proportionality assumption is dropped, since a reduction in hours may now affect the marginal product per hour of an additional employee, and hence the firm's demand for workers. **If decreasing returns to hours dominate, a reduction in hours will increase the contribution per hour of an additional worker, and so will increase the demand for labor. If the opposite is true, as when, for example, setup costs are more important than fatigue effects, the demand for employees will be reduced by a reduction in hours.**

Production Model 4. Finally, in the more general case, where there may be not only diminishing returns to labor services in the production of output but also either diminishing or increasing returns to hours and employment in providing effective labor input or labor services, a variety of possibilities are present. In the Keynesian case, a reduction in hours will still yield an increase in the demand for employees, but the increase need no longer be proportionate. The answer depends upon how the two combine to create labor services, since these need to be kept constant if output is not to change in this model. **Hence, if a reduction in hours has a more (less) severe effect on effective labor services than does a reduction in number of employees, a less (more) than proportionate increase in number of employees is required to maintain output.** In the neoclassical case, the direction of the effect on demand for employees depends (as in the other neoclassical models considered here) on the effect of hours reduction on the average contribution per hour of an additional employee. **Here, a variety of outcomes is possible. But if the effect on average contribution is positive, there is likely to be a positive effect on employment as well.**

This review of some simple models commonly used in the analysis of work time reduction shows how sensitive the predicted results are to assumptions. The Keynesian model (which rules out any reduction in output, despite hours reduction) generally yields more positive employment effects than does the neoclassical case (which does allow output to fall).

It is interesting to note that diminishing returns to hours implies a greater gain to employment in the neoclassical model than would be obtained with increasing returns. The opposite is true in the Keynesian regime. The difference is that in the Keynesian case the larger the potential drop in output due to hours reduction, the larger the increase in employment needed to restore output to its original level and thus satisfy the Keynesian constraint. In the neoclassical model, on the other hand, the issue turns on the effect of hours reduction on the average hourly product of a new worker: only if this is increased will employment gain. Hence, the smaller the drop in effective labor input as hours decline (and thus the larger the increase in the contribution of an hour's work), the more likely the employer is to increase employment.

EFFECTS WITH VARIABLE HOURLY COMPENSATION AND PRICES

The analysis of the neoclassical case becomes still more complicated and less determinate when the effects of hours reduction on the hourly compensation of labor and the price of final output are allowed to influence employment. Now, the rule used above (that the marginal product of labor per hour remains constant) must be replaced with a more stringent condition: that any increase in the ratio of hourly compensation to price resulting from hours reduction be matched by an increase in this marginal product.[6] (This is necessary to maintain equality of this marginal product with the ratio of wage to price.) But with capital stock and other inputs fixed by assumption, it follows (using the assumption of diminishing returns to labor input) that the marginal product of labor can be increased only by reducing the amount of labor employed. Hence, allowing for effects on the wage-price ratio may well yield a more pessimistic expectation of the impact of hours reduction on employment.

It is difficult to be more precise here. The discussion in the preceding chapter indicated that a reduction in hours is likely to yield an increase in wages, or at least in hourly compensation. However, there was considerable uncertainty about the likely *size* of that result. Because of both this uncertainty about employer reactions and the uncertainty introduced here by considering just a few commonly used microeconomic models of employment effects, one cannot predict the size of the employment impacts of wage increases induced by hours reduction. (Although few economists would predict that, in this neoclassical framework, a reduction in hours accompanied by an increase in wages sufficiently large to maintain intact the purchasing power of the workers would yield an employment gain: employment losses are much more likely.[7])

Moreover, another complication must also be considered: the impact of wage increases may be at least partially offset by price increases in this microeconomic framework. Recall that profit maximization requires that the firm compare changes in the sales revenue obtained from hiring more labor with its cost, and that sales revenue is a product of price and quantity sold. Hence, if a reduction in hours not only yields an increase in hourly wages but also an increase in the price of the product, some offset to the wage increase is obtained. Conventional microeconomic theory tells us that an increase in price depends, first, on the extent to which a reduction in hours yields a reduction in output and, second, on the extent to which the output reduction yields higher prices.

This second effect is of course inversely related to the price elasticity of demand (the percentage change in output associated with a percentage change in price). It will be very small or nonexistent when the firm is a price taker (as when it is one of many producing a homogeneous product). Then, a reduction in a firm's output does not influence industry price. But it may be significant when the firm is a price maker (as when it is producing a differentiated product or when it exerts a degree of market control). It will also be significant when hours reduction is imposed on an entire industry, and output is reduced. Then even if no one firm can influence price, a reduction in industry supply will be expected to increase the industry price. (Effects on the general price level are considered in the next chapter.)

The predicted microeconomic effect of a reduction in hours per worker on a firm's demand for employees is thus highly dependent on the microeconomic model chosen and on the forecast response of wage and price. Either declines or increases in the firm's employment are plausible outcomes.

DYNAMIC CONSIDERATIONS

A more realistic assessment of the microeconomic effects of hours reduction on employment generation must also consider the way the employer is likely to take into account future effects of his actions. The analysis to this point has been instantaneous, considering effects on the current value of the marginal product. But hiring employees has consequences that persist over time, since there are sizable hiring, screening, and training costs when employees are added, and there may be significant dismissal costs when they are let go. Moreover, there is likely to be a learning period when the new employee's production has not reached expected performance. (This cost may, of course, be considered part of the training cost.) Hence, employers must make estimates of their future employment needs, as well as of their present demand, in making their hiring decisions.

If hours reduction occurs at a time of stable, full employment, future uncertainty may not be an important factor, but it can be quite important under other circumstances. As the economy comes out of a recession, for example, many employers respond to increased consumer demand by introducing overtime hours rather than by hiring more workers. This typically produces demands to share the work. But if the underlying cause of employers' reluctance to hire new workers is uncertainty about future demand, then a rule that forces them to reduce hours of work may simply lead them to turn down consumer orders rather than hire new people. This could have unfortunate macroeconomic effects for the recovery process. On the other hand, if hours reduction is imposed during the beginning stages of a recession, this negative effect may not be so important. The employer is then deciding whether to lay off workers who are already trained, so that an investment decision need not be made.

Summary and Empirical Evidence

This review indicates that the prediction from microeconomic models of the effect of a policy of hours reduction on employment is at best mixed and depends on the model chosen. Hence, it not surprising that when employers in France, West Germany, and Great Britain were surveyed after an hours reduction and asked about the direct effect on their employment, a majority reported little or no positive impact.[8]

CHAPTER NINE

National Economic Effects

EFFECTS at the firm level on output, employment, wages and prices will affect national aggregates for the same variables. But the effect of hours reduction at that level is not the same as that predicted by simply aggregating impacts on firms, using the microeconomic models of the previous chapter. Changes in these variables will have indirect effects on interest rates, foreign exchange rates, the money supply, the deficit in national accounts, tax rates, and other macroeconomic variables. Moreover, decisions by firms to expand output and employment and to increase wages and prices will affect other firms, raising the demand for their products and increasing the cost of producing them. All these effects in turn affect output, employment, wages, and prices.

Such indirect impacts are of interest in themselves, but because of the relations among these variables, indirect or feedback effects must be considered even if one is simply interested in the effect of hours reduction on one variable, employment.[1]

The interpretation or prediction of these effects is no simple matter. There is now a variety of competing macroeconomic theories, and to trace out the effects of hours reduction in each of them would be a monumental task. Instead, the discussion here is restricted largely to theories which others have regarded as reasonable in analyzing the effects of hours reduction. Even with this restriction, a range of arguments needs to be considered. Writers on the macroeconomics of hours reduction differ on a number of important assumptions; the most basic division is between the Keynesian and neoclassical schools. Broadly speaking, Keynesian analysts emphasize aggregate demand as a determinant of total output, while neoclassical analysts take into account various cost elements as negative influences on output. But in addition to this two-way split, there are more specific issues that cut across this division (although the way they are handled is often correlated with whether the analyst is a Keynesian or a neoclassicist).

Large-Scale Macroeconomic Models

In large-scale macroeconomic models, much of the indirect effect of hours reduction occurs because of its impact on one or more of several variables.

INVESTMENT

Business investment is one of the most important determinants of economic activity in the short or medium run. Moreover, the determination of business investment is an issue that has long divided economists. Hence, it is not surprising that a key difference among macroeconomic models of hours reduction lies in the assumptions made about how it affects investment.

1. A reduction in hours is generally expected to reduce profits, and in some models this has a negative effect on investment.

2. A reduction in hours may increase consumer demand, especially if the reduction is accompanied by an increase both in employment and in hourly wages of employed workers. In Keynesian models, the influence of demand is given an important role in the determination of investment and output.

3. Reduced hours may increase labor costs, which can lower business profits. A lower profit level may reduce the flow of funds needed for investment.

4. In some models, an increase in labor costs creates an incentive to purchase labor-saving machinery, which would tend to enhance investment.

5. In some models, the rate of capacity utilization in industry has a positive effect on investment. Hours reduction, accompanied by an increase in employment, may increase capacity utilization: this would be an expected result in one-man-one-machine models of output, in which a reduction in hours does not ease the capacity utilization problem, while an increase in employment exacerbates it. In these models, lack of capacity creates a positive incentive to invest in new capacity.

6. But a reduction in capacity available for production reduces profits, and in some models this tends to decrease investment.

7. If employment gains do not offset hours reductions and output is reduced, then if the demand for investment is a function of output, investment demand is also reduced.

8. Higher interest rates reduce investment in some models, and these rates are (in some models) increased by the inflationary effects of hours reduction.

9. International flows of capital may be included as determinants of investment. If they are, the rate of return to capital may be more relevant to investment than is the flow of domestic profits. Moreover, changes in investment can occur more swiftly if investment can be augmented by capital imports or diminished by capital flight. Then, a reduction in profits consequent upon a reduction in hours may have a negative effect on investment.

WAGES AND PRICES

Changes in wages and prices at the national level will also affect both money and real output, in some models.

1. Earlier chapters suggested several ways in which, at the microlevel of the industry or firm, shorter hours might contribute to higher wages and prices. A general reduction in hours might exert upward pressure on wages and prices for the same reasons. For example, increased employment may lead to higher money wages.

2. In some models, a capacity constraint becomes operative as hours decline and employment increases, raising wages and prices.

3. Lags can play an important role. If wages rise before employment, then an excess of demand over supply may act to raise prices.

4. Still other models assign a wage-determining role to the capacity of the employer to pay. This acts as a constraint on wage increases resulting from hours reduction.

INTEREST RATES AND THE MONETARY SECTOR

If hours reduction results in higher prices, an increase in interest rates may result. This is likely if the central banking authorities do not expand the money supply to accommodate higher prices.[2]

FOREIGN EXCHANGE RATES AND INTERNATIONAL CAPITAL FLOWS

Hours reduction may affect the value of a nation's currency.

1. If shorter hours mean higher domestic prices, the result may be an increase in imports and a reduction of exports, and this may eventually reduce the value of the currency.

2. If hours reduction results in higher interest rates, this may help to attract international capital and so tend to raise interest rates (but perhaps with negative effects on the trade balance).

DOMESTIC FISCAL EFFECTS

1. There may be some reduction in government spending if hours reduction reduces the number of unemployed. This could occur if there were reductions in the outflow of unemployment insurance benefits and welfare payments. (This saving is minimized if work sharers receive a proportionate share of their unemployment benefit, as they may do under a short-time compensation plan.)

2. On the other hand, insofar as hours reduction yields an output loss, and insofar as tax revenues are dependent on output, government revenues will be reduced. Hence, the net effect on government finances depends both on whether hours reduction reduces unemployment and on whether it also reduces output.

Simulation of Macroeconomic Models

This listing of some major ways in which hours reduction can have macroeconomic effects brings out the difficulties of making unconditional forecasts of the impact of hours reduction. Moreover, economists differ not only on the effect of hours reduction on these and other variables but also on the relative importance of such variables in determining aggregate output and demand. And even if there were agreement, it would be a difficult task to work through all the indirect effects of hours reduction on the economy.

One approach to solving this last problem, however, is provided by the simulation method—that is, by simulating the effects of hours reduction in a large-scale model of the economy. Here, one starts with a model that posits a large number of causal relations among economic variables. The model also includes a numerical estimate of the size of each of these effects. Typically, the model chosen is one that is well established and has been employed in forecasting or planning a national economy. One then inserts numerical values for each of the economic variables, usually based on recent experience. Then, if hours of work appears as one of the variables in the model, one can change its value and observe, or simulate, the consequences for all the other variables directly or indirectly affected by hours reduction.

In practice, many of the direct effects of hours reduction discussed in earlier chapters are not incorporated in these standard models. As a result, it is customary to introduce these effects by making additional assumptions about them—that is, by assuming that hours reduction is accompanied by a specified change in one or more of the following variables: the extent to which overtime or other variations in labor supply offset the reduction in hours; the extent to which productivity or other changes affect the amount of hours required per unit of output; and direct, or first-round, changes in money wages per hour, unit labor costs, employment, and prices.[3]

These simulations have other limitations. Since they are very costly and time consuming, it is customary to simulate the model just once, or perhaps with two or three iterations. But there are, as noted above, a number of microeconomic assumptions that have to be made: as we saw in earlier chapters, there is little consensus about how firms, unions, and workers will react to hours reduction, so that a variety of plausible assumptions can be made. Since a range of assumptions have to be made on a number of issues, the number of combinations of possible assumptions is large. These cannot be explored because of the expense. Moreover, each model reflects a given macroeconomic analysis. As a result, one can expect wide variation in the estimated effects of hours reduction and considerable uncertainty about the extent to which variation is caused by macroeconomic or micro-economic assumptions.

Nevertheless, a review of these simulations is helpful. Such a review is provided by Winter van Ginneken, who summarized a number of large-scale simulations of the effects of hours reductions carried out independently in West Germany, France, the United Kingdom, Belgium, and the Netherlands in the early 1980s.[4] Through a close examination of the different models, he was able to ascertain some of the reasons for divergence or similarities in their predictions.

Van Ginneken concluded: "Nearly all models make it clear that there is a trade-off between economic growth and employment, if the work week is reduced. The reason behind this trade-off is the relationship between inflation and economic growth. All models show a significant increase in inflation, particularly when wages are fully compensated. Inflation also tends to be higher when production capacity is reduced, because this increases the cost of capital." There are other deleterious effects. "Full wage compensation tends to boost private consumption at the expense of exports." But in any event, "exports tend to grow more slowly than in the base run even when wages are reduced in proportion to the reduced work week."

On the positive side, the national deficit is improved through hours reduction if it is not accompanied by an increase in hourly wages. This occurs because of a reduction in unemployment and related benefits. If wages are increased, the same benefit is observed in some models, but the deficit is increased in others. In general, the aggregate of real national consumption, investment, and production is reduced by a cut in hours in these simulations, while consumer prices are higher. Exceptions are found in the case of investment, when, in most Keynesian models, demand is allowed to be a determinant of investment, but costs are not: then the simple accelerator effect of increased demand raises investment.

However, while the results show that because of hours reduction "real income per wage earner is usually lower than in the base run," most of these simulations show some gain in employment. Table 9.1 gives the estimates of the effects of hours reduction on employment. The top half of the table gives estimates for reductions in excess of 8 percent, the bottom half for smaller reductions. Effects are expressed in terms of elasticities: the

TABLE 9.1. Elasticities of Employment with Respect to Reduction in Weekly Working Hours

Country and Model	Elasticity Range[a]	Reduction
	Over 8% Reduction	
Netherlands		
Vintaf model	−.193 to −.168	2.5% a year, 1979–83
Freia model	.125 to .488	2.5% a year, 1983–86
Belgium		
Maribel model	.348	2% a year, 1983–86, on top of 1% trend
France		
DMS model	.582 to .633	2% a year, 1983–86, on top of trend
	Reductions of 8% and under	
United Kingdom		
Treasury model	.048 to .280	
West Germany		
Henize model	.680 to .840	
France		
DMS model	.325 to .451	
Metric model	.593	

Source: Calculated from data in van Ginneken, "Employment and the Reduction of the Workweek," tables 4 and 5. Characteristics of the models are given in van Ginneken and sources cited there.
[a]Percentage increase in employment per 1% reduction in hours.

percentage increase in employment per 1 percent reduction in hours per worker.

Variation among the models in simulated employment effects broadly corresponds to the differences in the economic philosophy that underlies the model. Fairly good effects are found in the most Keynesian models, the French DMS model, and John Henize's model for West Germany. The most neoclassical model, the Dutch Vintaf, yields the most negative assessment. The model that gives the most important role to the monetary sector (allowing the central bank to follow a tight money policy when hours reduction ignites inflationary forces) also shows fairly poor results.

Within each model, variation is also produced when different assumptions are employed. For each set of simulations, the highest and lowest employment effects are given. Variation within the model is due to several factors. Some estimate the model with and without the assumption that wages are raised to compensate for hours reduction. Some assume that capital utilization is reduced by hours reduction, and some do not. And the British model simulates the effect of hours reduction with and without an accommodative monetary policy. These different assumptions will influence the simulated effect on employment:

1. If one assumes that production capacity is not reduced by hours reduction (so that employment is easily substituted for hours per worker), then employment effects are larger. In practice, this means that one assumes that shift work can be used as a good substitute for day work in the economy.[5]

2. If monetary policy is assumed to accommodate price rises caused by hours reduction, a larger employment gain is generally predicted than if money is tight.

3. The effect of wage increases that compensate for declines in hours on employment depend on the model used. They have a negative effect in the Vintaf and British models but a positive effect in the DMS model in France and in Henize's model for Germany. This can be explained by the fact that the latter two are Keynesian models: in such models, higher wages function largely as a positive influence on consumer and investment demand.

Overall, these results indicate some significantly positive effects on employment in most of the models, though at the cost of other macroeconomic variables (including output) of concern to the policymaker. It is worth stressing, though, that the employment effects estimated in these macroeconomic models are less than those obtained from the microeconomic assumptions made about the immediate effects of hours reduction on the hiring decisions of managers.

Moreover, van Ginneken discusses evidence that even these simulation results are too optimistic. When the French actually did reduce work time (by one hour per week, in 1982), the employment gains—according to the French government's own estimates—were only 10–20 percent of those predicted by the model. Part of this gap may be due to the exclusion from the survey of effects of nonindustrial employment, but even when a generous correction was made for this omission, the observed gain is only about half as great as that predicted by the model.[6] One reason for this poor result is that employment growth was mostly confined to large enterprises, especially those where there was a possibility of adding another shift. Smaller enterprises tended to let production lapse, rather than add staff. Many enterprises increased the work pace or maintained production without an increase in employment, despite reduction in hours. Overall, it appears that the microeconomic assumptions made in these macroeconomic simulations were too optimistic.[7]

Despite these discouraging results from earlier simulations, J. D. Whitley and R. A. Wilson simulated hours reduction for Great Britain using a number of models of the British economy.[8] They assumed a 5 percent reduction in normal hours and varying degrees of overtime leakage. For those simulations in which hours declined by about 4 percent (nine out of the twelve cases they examined), the employment elasticity of actual hours reduction ranged from .18 to .92 after one year and from −.4 to .58 after four years. Output varied hardly at all in the first years in most models. After four years, half the simulations showed declines of about 1 percent or more. Domestic prices rose significantly in many of the models, by as much as 14 percent after four years. However, there was a range of estimates: about two-thirds of the simulations showed price increases of 3 percent or less. Estimates of the effect on the exchange rate also varied widely.

A Simplified Model

As an alternative to the simulation of large-scale models, one can devise a smaller, simplified model specifically designed to determine the effects of hours reduction under plausible conditions. Here, one begins by asking a series of more specific questions. Is there indeed a constellation of microeconomic and macroeconomic circumstances that are producing and will produce over the next several years undesirably high unemployment? If so, what are these circumstances? And how will a state-ordered reduction in working hours affect these conditions? Will it reduce unemployment? A model is then developed to answer these questions.

There are costs to using this approach. A small-scale model tailored for a specific use must omit much of the detail of the large models considered above. But an important compensating advantage is that one can more easily incorporate judgments on important issues, such as whether an unemployment crisis is due to inadequate aggregate demand or is more closely related to the high cost of certain types of labor relative to productivity. Specific effects of hours reduction on variables such as productivity may also be introduced more readily here.

Perhaps the most pessimistic assessment of the causes of unemployment is offered in a speculative discussion by British economist Richard Layard, in a colloquium on European stagflation.[9] In the course of his discussion of the use of wage subsidies to reduce unemployment, Layard asked whether the Thatcher government believed that a high rate of unemployment was necessary to keep down inflation and to pursue other goals. If this was true, then whether or not the government was correct in its assessment of the beneficial effects of unemployment, the result of a successful policy to reduce unemployment will be that the government will change other policies designed to restore unemployment to its former level, perhaps by adopting a still more stringent monetary policy. Under these circumstances, a reduction in hours will not reduce unemployment—it will simply reduce the purchasing power of the employed. An equally pessimistic result is obtained if one assumes that trade union leaders will raise wages to compensate for any income reductions that may result from hours reduction.

A more moderate approach was offered in a very interesting paper on hours reduction by Norwegian economist Michael Hoel. Hoel also began by asking why unemployment persists. He answered by citing four overlapping reasons why "expansive fiscal or monetary policy . . . can . . . not be used today to increase labor demand": inflation, balance of payments, government budget balance, and the fact that unemployment is classical, not Keynesian.[10] (Here, Hoel defined classical unemployment as resulting from a real wage that is too high to clear the market, given the capital stock and the number of people wishing to work.) He then devised a very simple macroeconomic model, which incorporated these considerations. This model indicates that, if labor costs are increased by a reduction in hours, output will fall. The net effect on employment "will depend on . . . how labor productivity changes, on the degree of wage compensation, . . . and on how much the operating time of capital is reduced." Hoel then obtained the striking conclusion that "for reasonable combinations of productivity change, wage compensation, and reduction in operating time employment may *decline* if the working time is reduced" (emphasis added).[11]

In summary, various attempts to use macroeconomic analysis to estimate employment and other effects of work sharing at the national level do not substantially change the mixed assessment derived from a consideration of effects at the level of the firm, presented in the last chapter.

Conclusions for Part 2

A government policy of hours reduction is unlikely to prove an effective way of dealing with a medium-term problem of high unemployment.

1. Legislation designed to achieve this purpose may not be effective in reducing hours to the desired extent. This is likely to be a less important objection if a reduction in the standard workweek is accompanied by a large rise in the overtime penalty premium and by a stepped-up enforcement effort.

2. Employers will at first respond to a reduction in hours by hoarding less labor and by speeding up their employees. In the longer run, though,

labor hoarding will be a less important effect, while more negative productivity effects of hours reduction, such as a less efficient utilization of personnel and machinery, will become more important.

3. Labor costs per hour are likely to increase. There will be an upward pressure on money wages. Moreover, fringe benefit costs will have to be spread over fewer working hours, further increasing costs per hour. The effect on labor costs per unit of product are not so clear: possible gains in productivity per hour (associated with less labor hoarding and greater worker effort) could act as offsets to higher hourly costs in the short run. The industrial relations climate as well as technical conditions in industry will help to determine the extent to which labor costs rise as hours are reduced.

4. Neoclassical microeconomic theory predicts that the impact of hours reduction on employment will (in the absence of an increase in hourly compensation) depend on the effect on the marginal product of an hour of an additional worker's input. But this will be dependent on production technology and on the net effect on labor effort and productivity. And there is really no consensus on these important issues. Higher compensation per hour resulting from hours reduction will, in most microeconomic models, induce employers to reduce the amount of labor they employ. More favorable results are obtained in Keynesian models, but these are not widely accepted for medium-term analyses.

5. Similarly, positive or negative employment effects of hours reduction can be obtained in a macroeconomic analysis, depending on the choice of model. Thus, if one assumes that hours reduction, followed by a compensatory increase in hourly wages, yields higher labor income, one may see a positive impact on employment in the Keynesian model, which emphasizes purchasing power, but a negative effect in the neoclassical model, which gives labor costs an important role. There appears to be somewhat greater agreement that hours reduction is likely to have adverse effects on other macroeconomic variables, such as inflation, the balance of payments, and interest rates.

6. Hence, hours reduction cannot be recommended as a way of dealing with medium-term unemployment. Its effect on employment may be positive, but this is not certain. And it is very likely to have a number of negative side effects on the economy.

7. This negative assessment does not, of course, apply to efforts by management and labor to deal in a cooperative way with medium-term declines in demand for the product of a firm or industry by reducing hours. Under some circumstances, such work sharing may be an appropriate response, even in the medium term. Furthermore, this assessment does not in any way imply a negative view of hours flexibility as a way of dealing with *short-term* fluctuations in labor demand.

PART III

Long-Term Effects of Reduced Work Time

CHAPTER TEN

Two Scenarios

THE ANALYSIS in the previous chapters considered the medium-term effects of work time reduction when it is adopted as a work-sharing device to deal with unemployment. But work time reduction has longer term implications, which go well beyond these effects. Moreover, a reduction in hours can occur for reasons other than a desire to share limited employment opportunities. Dramatic reductions in work time have occurred in the United States over the past century and a half as a result of the workings of the private labor market, and future reductions need not wait upon new work-sharing legislation.

The following chapters consider the long-term consequences of a major, permanent reduction in work time. Obviously, the effects of a decrease in work time would be muted if the reduction were very small, say, one hour a week. In order to point up the importance of work time reduction, a more significant level of cuts—in the 20-25 percent range—are assumed in the discussion below.[1] It will be argued that the *effect* of work time reduction will depend critically on its *cause*. For this reason, it is useful to consider briefly some circumstances that might give rise to hours reduction, before turning to a discussion of its impact.

Causes of Work Time Reduction

EXPLANATIONS FROM THE PAST

The basic explanation offered by economists of past reductions in work time is that increases in wage rates increased the demand of the American worker for leisure. A higher wage raises the income of the worker, and higher income raises his demand for leisure, along with his demand for consumer goods. True, the wage hike also raises the opportunity cost of taking leisure (the amount of consumer goods sacrificed per hour taken), and this would in itself tend to reduce the demand for leisure. But if hours do in fact decline as wages rise, this can be interpreted as evidence that the income effect of a wage increase is greater than the substitution effect.

For a century or more, this plausible explanation seemed to fit the data—there was an upward trend in real hourly wages and a downward trend in hours worked. However, as noted in chapter 1, the post-World War II period did not see a continuation of this pattern. Although real hourly wages rose rapidly, annual work time declined quite slowly. One simple explanation for this new pattern is that, once hours reach the forty-hour level, workers are relatively contented, and the marginal value of additional leisure to them is small: their demand for increased leisure as income rises is weak. Under these circumstances, the income effect of further wage increases no longer dominates the substitution effect, and hours remain stable.[2] This rather simplistic explanation would predict no further demands for reductions in work time in the future as real hourly wages rise still further.

A different argument tries to identify specific factors that might account for the changed behavior in the postwar period and to use empirical research to verify these hypotheses. Econometric analysis of time-series data has shown that two other labor supply developments—later entrance into the labor force and earlier retirement from it—can explain the leveling-off of hours. The phenomena of the baby boom and the education revolution (i.e., an upsurge in birth rates and higher educational expectations) greatly increased child-rearing costs of the average American male and contributed to a slowdown in hours reduction, especially in the first several decades of this period. In more recent years, the increased cost of providing a much better living standard for an older population that is larger, retires earlier, and lives longer helps to explain the continued relative stability of work time.[3]

In addition to these influences on the overall trend in hours, there has been pressure on sectors of the labor market or on the general labor market at a given time. The principal example of the latter is the pressure to reduce hours during periods of slack demand in the labor market. Hours of work fell dramatically in the Depression of the 1930s and have also declined during each of the recessions since World War II. These declines in hours were followed by increases in subsequent recoveries, so that the long-term impact on work schedules is not clear. One can argue, for example, that the hours reduction induced by the Great Depression made it easier for employers and legislators to accept a forty-hour week in the more prosperous years that followed. Or one can maintain that work time would have been reduced in any case, as a result of the upward trend in hourly wages.

The increased labor force participation of women has also tended to reduce working hours in the sectors in which women constitute a major portion of the work force. For example, about 70 percent of voluntary part-timers are women. And the average workweek of women employed full time is 8 percent below that of male full-timers.

Finally, welfare state institutions may have had some impact on work schedules. This impact is limited under the American system because benefits are generally confined to those who are not working at all or, at most, are working part time. They are typically small or unavailable to the working poor, and hence will have a minimal effect on the standard, full-time workweek. There may be indirect effects, however. For example, some natural fathers may allow the welfare state to take responsibility for the support of their children and the mothers of these children (through the Aid to Families of Dependent Children program). The fathers may still have to enter the full-time labor market in order to provide for their own sustenance, but may be able to obtain sufficient income with a shorter workweek. And of course the higher marginal tax rates required by the welfare state provide a potential disincentive for all employed people.

LOOKING TO THE FUTURE

At the present time, there is very little pressure for work time reduction. A recent survey of U.S. employees by the Department of Labor found that only one in thirteen would prefer to work fewer hours if it meant a proportional reduction in pay.[4] But several factors could lead to future reductions in work time.

1. It is possible that the causes of the slowdown in work time reduction that have been operative over the past forty years will lose some of their force. The two labor supply trends—later entrance into the labor force and earlier retirement from it—may not continue. These trends have become very expensive, producing considerable resistance to further reductions in the length of a working life. Much of the financing for these reductions has come from intergenerational transfers—support for the education of the young and pensions and other contributions for the maintenance of the retired aged—and the working age population has already given indications that it would prefer to contain such costs. If such resistance is successfully mounted (so that, for example, the trend toward early retirement is ended or even reversed), the easing of pressure on the typical American employee might produce a return to the longer term pattern of declines in the annual work time of the employed population, as wages rise.

2. Growth in productivity and real wages may also influence the course of hours reduction. As we have seen, the simple model of labor supply in which higher real hourly wage rates yield shorter hours of work has not predicted well over the past forty years or so. However, statistical estimation of time-series data does show that hours per worker are responsive to changes in the real hourly wage, *if other factors are held constant*.[5] In consequence, a rapid increase in productivity and hence in real hourly wages should be considered as a *contributing* factor to hours reduction.

Certainly, it is easier to accept a forecast of substantial hours reduction if one also forecasts growth in hourly wages sufficiently great that the living standards of the work force would not suffer an absolute decline.

3. Perhaps the most plausible way for a substantial reduction in working hours to occur is for there to be a period of persistently high unemployment. This could provide the spur needed for a national hours reduction policy, a policy that might be retained as a permanent feature of the American labor market.

4. Higher female labor force participation may also contribute to a reduction in working hours. As the employment of women in traditionally male jobs becomes more common, one may see a change in the standard, full-time workweek to one that better conforms to the preferences of women.[6] (More speculatively, if males take on a larger share of housework and child care, they too may develop a preference for a shorter work schedule.)

5. One can also speculate about the future effect of the welfare state on work time. It is of course difficult to say whether there will be a continuation of welfare state trends (such as an increase in the progressivity of taxes or an increase in welfare relative to the average hourly wage) or whether new policies, such as more assistance to the working poor, will be adopted. American opinion is clearly divided on all these issues, and one can also question the effect of such changes on work schedules. There is little doubt that they reduce the financial incentives of individuals to provide effort. But they do not reduce the social cost of hours reduction. Under welfare state conditions, a work time reduction is likely to raise everybody's tax rate (compare the discussion of the effects of hours reduction on tax rates in chapter 13). It is very difficult to predict whether political leaders will take such indirect effects into account when shaping an hours reduction policy.

Scenarios for Work Time Reduction

Hours reduction may then occur as a result of a number of different factors. The effect of hours reduction is expected to depend in large measure on the circumstances that accompany it. Hence, it is useful to describe the possible scenarios in which hours are reduced and then kept low. In the interest of brevity, however, only two scenarios of hours reduction are considered. In the first, the reduction is more or less consistent with the preferences of employees—they are willing to give up income to obtain a significant increase in leisure. The mechanism of change may be national legislation or union bargaining, but this collective decision making is not greatly at variance with individual preferences. It is assumed that this scenario is accompanied by high growth in productivity and real hourly wages, so that hours reduction has the effect of "splitting the melon" of economic growth between greater leisure and higher income. This scenario would, in broad outline, replicate the historical movement toward long-term hours reduction in the United States.[7]

In the second scenario, hours are reduced to a significantly greater extent than would be dictated by individual preferences expressed in a free market. Legislation and other collective influences are given the major role. In the interest of comparison, it is assumed that average hours per job are reduced to the same extent as in the first scenario (although the number of people seeking employment varies between the two scenarios).

The mechanisms by which hours are reduced are not discussed in detail. The discussion in chapter 5 describes a number of difficulties in reducing hours through legislation and other collective means: not all workers are covered by the legislation; enforcement of the law remains a problem; overtime can be increased to avoid the effects of the law; and so on. Moreover, the force of these difficulties is greater in the longer term setting than it might be in the medium term, characterized by high unemployment. For example, employers and employees are expected, with practice, to become adept at avoiding the effects of the law. Hence, the assumption that the same reduction takes place in this scenario as in the first, where the reduction is voluntary, necessarily makes the tacit assumption that a major effort is also made to make the law more effective (e.g., by broadening coverage, increasing the budget for enforcement, and raising overtime penalty premia). It is also assumed, for convenience, that hours reduction in this second scenario occurs in the face of slow productivity growth. Hence, increased leisure is accompanied by a reduction in income.

Two additional reference scenarios are also posited. In the third, productivity growth and other factors are the same as in the first, but hours are not reduced: workers prefer still more income to an increase in leisure. Similarly, in the fourth scenario, productivity and other variables are the same as in the second scenario, but the government does not intervene to reduce hours. One can then discuss the effect of hours reduction in the first scenario as the difference between economic and social conditions in the first and third scenarios. The effect of work time reduction in the second scenario is the difference between conditions in that scenario and in the fourth scenario.

CHAPTER ELEVEN

Labor Efficiency

A LONG-TERM REDUCTION in working hours will influence the amount of labor used in the economy, which will in turn influence national output. These effects are assessed in this and the next chapter. The analysis follows the conventional modern economic treatment, in which output is a function of capital and labor. Effects on labor supply and labor utilization are considered in this chapter, while effects on capital stock and the utilization of this stock are analyzed in the next chapter. (Because of the importance of energy and raw materials as complementary factors of production, these effects are considered in a brief discussion in chapter 13.) All these effects are considered in the context of the overall impact of hours reduction on national output.

Labor Supply Changes and Employment Levels

The most important and controversial issue here is the effect of hours reduction on the amount of labor utilized in production. To resolve this, we must first consider the relation between changes in labor supply and changes in the amount of labor utilized and ask: Will a change in labor supply eventually yield a change in labor demand of roughly the same size? If changes in labor supply can be equated with changes in labor demand, one can proceed by predicting effects of hours reduction on labor supply and then considering the effects of a reduction in labor input on national output.

But if one instead holds that the demand for labor is not responsive to changes in labor supply—so that a reduction in hours per worker would simply reduce the number of unemployed workers, with relatively little effect on aggregate labor utilized—a very different type of analysis is needed. This second approach is popular with those who argue that hours of work should be permanently reduced by law because our economy will not be able to provide sufficient demand for expected increases in labor supply even in the long run. These critics cite labor force growth as well as the technical possibilities for automation and other labor-saving devices and point to the present level of unemployment as evidence that there already has been a shortfall of economic growth.

This perspective is rejected by economists who believe that an expansion of the supply of labor in the long run yields greater production and increased demand for labor, not higher unemployment. In fact, the American labor force grew from two million in 1800 to over one hundred million in 1987; but capital investment adapted to this enormous labor supply growth by creating a vast number of new jobs—to the point where all but a small fraction of the work force is employed. And for those who are not impressed by this experience, there are a number of specific reasons that can be adduced for not adopting the work-sharing theory as a basis for future policy.

1. The American labor force will not be growing so rapidly in the future as it did in the recent past, since it has begun to reflect the lower birth rates of the past two decades. A study commissioned by the U.S. Department of Labor, *Workforce 2000,* predicted that "the labor force, which exploded by 2.9 percent per year in the 1970's, will be expanding by only 1 percent annually in the 1990's."[1] Moreover, the reduction in labor force growth would be much greater if it were not for immigration to the United States—immigrants are forecast by *Workforce 2000* to account for 22 percent of net labor force growth from now to the turn of the century. This immigration rate is under the control of the U.S. government (inasmuch as both laws controlling immigration and the enforcement of these laws are a function of government). For those who feel that a reduction in labor force growth is needed to prevent unemployment, a more restrictive immigration policy provides an alternative.

2. There are a number of areas in which the demand for labor is likely to expand in the years ahead. Many of these are in the service industries, in which mechanization is difficult and which tend to receive a larger share of income as the nation becomes more affluent. Examples include health care and care for the aged; protection (including security forces, the criminal justice system, and the penal system); child care (required by the increased proportion of working women); and recreation and restaurant and fast-food facilities. This brief list could be greatly extended. The point is that, despite the mechanization of many routinized jobs, there remain enormous needs for labor if we intend to provide an affluent life-style in the years ahead.

3. New technologies create new jobs as well as eliminate others. The course that mechanization takes reflects the relative scarcity of labor as well as the exogenous progress of scientific discovery. Some believe that opportunities for replacing labor are scarcer today because of the growth in the labor-intensive service industries, while others expect major technical

breakthroughs that would make it possible to eliminate millions of jobs, even in the service sector. But the progress of mechanization will depend in part upon the availability and costs of different types of labor, which help to determine the direction and speed of research to find labor substitutes.[2] Thus, *Workforce 2000* argued that even without hours restriction the predicted low rate of growth of the labor force may "force employers to use capital-intensive production systems."[3] According to this view, making labor artificially scarce by reducing hours of work would very likely spur new research efforts to find new ways to reduce labor demand. A related argument is that, in the long run, the machinery to employ the expanded labor force is produced by labor. Hence, reducing the labor supply (by reducing hours of work) will in the long run curtail the supply of new jobs. (This argument is explored more fully in chapter 12.)

Of course, it is possible that the confidence of many economists is misplaced—that in spite of the underlying technological and social demands for labor, institutional contradictions in our capitalist economic system will somehow prevent that demand from being made effective, and the economy will enter a permanent depression. This pessimistic scenario will not be pursued further here. The assumption made below is that a change in the quantity of labor supplied will be translated into a roughly equal change in the quantity of labor utilized, in the long run.

Effects on Labor Supply

It is useful to think of the long-run supply of effective labor input as having several dimensions:

Effective labor input supplied = total hours (hours per worker × number of workers seeking employment) × effort per hour of work × economic efficiency of effort × quality of work force.

Total hours are the total number of hours supplied to the labor market. Effort per working hour is a function of the physical fatigue of the worker, but also of the extent to which the worker is bored, tired, hostile, or indifferent to the work and the extent to which the employment environment permits or encourages less than full effort. The quality of the worker depends upon skills, and hence upon education and on-the-job training. The economic efficiency of the input is determined by such factors as the relative cost of hiring, screening, and training the worker; daily setup costs; and problems of supervising, coordinating, and arranging communication among workers.

NUMBER OF WORKING HOURS SUPPLIED

The effect of an hours reduction policy on total hours supplied to the economy will depend very much on whether the policy is in accord with the wishes of the individual workers who compose the work force. If, as in the second scenario, this condition is not met, an increase in the number of job seekers is likely, partially offsetting the effect of the reduction in hours. A decline in real income per employed worker in this scenario would encourage increased female labor force participation; increased self-employment and moonlighting; and some switching of part-time to full-time employment.[4]

But if a national policy of hours reduction is consistent with preferences for income and leisure, as in the first scenario, the effects on the number of job seekers will obviously be less. A reduction in the full-time workweek does, though, open up employment opportunities to those (housewives, students, and the retired) for whom a forty-hour week is too demanding and who find part-time jobs an unattractive option. Hence, some increase in the number of job seekers is plausible even in this first scenario.[5]

EFFORT PER HOUR OF WORK

Effective labor supply can also be augmented by an increase in the amount of effort workers supply per hour on the job. An increase in hourly effort very often can be obtained when hours are reduced, but the question is to what extent, if any, the physical possibilities opened up by a reduction in fatigue are exploited in the form of higher productivity. (Compare the discussion in chapter 6.) This must depend critically on the scenario in which hours are reduced. If they are reduced by law, despite widespread interest by individual workers in maintaining their material living standard (as in the second scenario), successful productivity bargaining at the plant level might well yield a significant increase in effort per hour in return for a smaller loss of income. The rationale for this forecast is much the same as that offered in the shorter term analysis in chapter 6: a reduction in work time is expected to make work less oppressive, thereby reducing the disutility of work effort; it is also expected to reduce income, thereby increasing the marginal utility of income to employees. The theory predicts that under these circumstances the typical worker would be more willing to trade additional work effort for additional income.

The long-term analysis does differ in some respects from the medium-term, though, since transitional effects are not important in the longer term. Any temporary, productivity-increasing "Hawthorne effects" would have vanished. On the other hand, labor and management would have had time to develop new skills and organizational technologies to better exploit the possibilities for increasing productivity in a shorter workday.[6] Finally, the specific industrial relations climate in which work time is reduced might be less important in the longer run, and so would be less likely to offset the underlying economic argument for expecting an increase in effort.

If hours are reduced in the first scenario, however, a similar argument cannot be made for expecting an increase in hourly effort. Indeed, if there is a general movement away from the work ethic and toward a more lei-surely life-style, one is more likely to observe *less* effort per hour as well as fewer hours worked. Some observers believe that this well describes the American work force as it moved from a forty-eight or longer workweek in the 1920s to the present workweek of forty hours or less.

In fact, a more significant decline in work effort might be observed in the future. In past years, any decline in the work ethic on the job that coincided with the gradual reduction in working hours was at least partly offset by the effect of reduced fatigue. This fatigue effect was said to be less important as workers went from a forty-eight- to a forty-hour workweek than was the case when, at an earlier time, the workweek was reduced from sixty or seventy hours. And it is likely to be still less important as the work-week is shortened further—and so to constitute a less important offset to any decline in the work ethic on the job. In any event, it is not obvious that if Americans voluntarily choose more leisure they will simultaneously choose to increase their work pace, reduce their break time, and so on.

The effect of hours reduction on effective labor input also depends on the form of the reduction. If most of it is taken in the form of more days and weeks off per year—maybe moving the United States up to the Euro-pean standard in this regard—the argument for an increase in effort is much weaker than if it is taken in the form of a six- or six-and-a-half-hour day. Here, too, the scenario is important. There is a strong trend toward taking time off in days rather than as fewer hours per day, and there is little reason to expect a departure from this trend in the first scenario. But if hours are reduced by law, and management and labor both want to mini-mize production loss by exploiting the possibilities of a reduced schedule, then a reduction in the workday, rather than more vacation time, might be the more attractive option. (Compare the discussion of leisure time mod-ules in chapter 13.)

EFFICIENCY OF LABOR UTILIZATION

The effect of work time reduction on effective labor input per hour also depends on such factors as hiring, screening, and training costs, and on the problems of managing communication and coordination among the work force. The judgment reached on these issues in the discussion of the medium-term in chapter 6 was somewhat mixed: they were assessed as unimportant in the very short run but as gradually increasing in significance over time. For example, if a short-term hours reduction meant that fewer workers were laid off during a recession, the company would actually have a gain in that it would not lose the training investments it had made in these workers. Later, though, the company would find that it had to train more people to maintain output, since each employee put in fewer hours. Similarly, it was argued that it was only in the long run that the use of layoffs rather than shorter hours enabled a company to take advantage of the savings in coordination and communications costs of working with a smaller labor force or the probable gains from concentrating output in more efficient production lines. Such major adjustments would not be possible in the short run.

But here we consider only the long-term effects, so that a simpler, less ambiguous set of conclusions can be drawn. In the absence of positive short-term offsets, one would expect only negative long-term effects—greater hiring, screening, training, communications, and coordination costs per hour of work. Again, the basic reasoning is very simple. These are all, essentially, costs per employee rather than costs per hour worked, and if one reduces the number of hours worked per employee, then one expects an increase in such costs per hour worked.

EVIDENCE FROM THE PART-TIME
LABOR MARKET

The case of voluntary part-time workers (i.e., those who seek a part-time schedule voluntarily) is instructive. Here we can observe long-run or equilibrium effects of shorter hours, free of the transitional effects emphasized in part 2. Evidence on the productivity of part-timers provides some basis for predicting the effects of short schedules, at least in the first scenario, where reduced work time is voluntary. There is a wealth of experience at the firm level with U.S. employers who employ at least some of their workers on part-week schedules. Over one-fifth of the jobs in the United States are held by part-timers.[7] This experience does not support an optimistic conclusion on the effects of a general reduction in hours. True, there are some jobs, especially those that are unusually boring or fatiguing, in which the hourly productivity of part-timers is reported to be superior to that of full-timers (often because of the increased effort per hour obtained with a shorter workday in such jobs). But labor market data indicate that part-timers are generally regarded as less productive than full-timers.

When hourly wage data are adjusted for differences in sex, race, education, experience, and other background factors, part-timers are paid only 70 percent of the full-time rate. Moreover, part-timers often do not receive the same fringe benefits as full-timers, so that straight wage comparisons underestimate the difference in total compensation. A major reason for their relatively poor pay is that part-timers are generally denied access to training and promotion opportunities and are largely confined to lower paying jobs. Over two-thirds of the wage gap has been found to be due to the fact that part-timers were disproportionately represented in poorly paid industries and occupations.

There are several economic explanations for this poor treatment of the part-timer, deriving from the economic inefficiency of using this type of worker in many jobs. The most basic reason is the fixed per employee costs that must be prorated over the term of employment. The shorter schedule of the part-timer means that investment in one of them will, ceteris paribus, have only about half the payoff as investment in a full-timer, discouraging employers from making such investments.[8] Moreover, if more workers must be hired to do the same amount of work, supervisory, communications, and coordination costs will be higher, making it more difficult for employees to find positions where complex, long-lasting interaction with other workers is essential. It can be significantly more difficult to resolve the coordination and communication problems when part-timers are used in sequential shifts. But in industries such as mining, manufacturing, and railroads, where capital-labor ratios are high and efficient capital utilization a key problem, it may make sense for part-timers to be used only if they can be employed in sequential shifts. Very little use of part-timers is made in blue collar jobs in these industries.[9]

The present gap in wage compensation between full-time and part-time employees may even underestimate the decline in efficiency that a further reduction in hours of work would bring. Part-timers are now used most heavily by employers in those jobs where they have a comparative advantage, least heavily where their use would be most inefficient. In many jobs in retail trade, recreation, and other service industries, the part-timer serves a real need. Whenever there are peaks and valleys of service demands over the course of the business day or week, or where there is a service demand for a few hours in the evening or on a weekend, the use of part-timers permits employers to match service needs and working hours. If employers were restricted to full-timers, they would have to choose between having too much labor during slack periods and losing sales during the peak hours. As one might expect, it is in these situations that we find a very high rate of part-time employment.

Part-timers, though often used in boring jobs and barred from promotion, are often better qualified in terms of background characteristics, such as education. The use of overqualified college students or housewives can sometimes overcome the other disadvantages of using part-timers, since a highly intelligent, well-educated employee can usually learn a job faster than a less qualified worker, with obvious benefits for the employer. For example, if an employee stays two years with a company (whether full or part time), then, if a job requires three months for a full-timer to learn but six months for a half-timer, the latter is at a distinct disadvantage in competing for the position. But if the pool of applicants for half-time jobs of this type is distinctly superior in quality, perhaps the employer can find half-timers who will be able to learn the work in just three months; then part-timers and full-timers will be competitive.

However, a very different result must be forecast if hours of work for all jobs are substantially reduced. Employers would no longer be able to cream the market for their short-hour jobs. Even more important, short-timers would not be confined to a relatively few positions where their schedules would cause the least problems (or where they would even be an advantage), but would instead be used in mainstream jobs, even in very complex situations—as production workers and technicians in capital-intensive industries and even, if hours reduction is truly general, as executives and professionals. This would very likely result in a significant reduction in efficiency.

Of course, one can challenge the notion that the lower wages paid to part-timers provides a good prediction of the effect of a general hours reduction. Advocates of the part-timer have argued that managers are prejudiced, or at least have not taken the trouble to investigate the potential benefits that these employees could bring to their enterprises. Economists will be perplexed by this argument, especially when applied to very competitive industries where work schedule discrimination could put a firm at a distinct disadvantage vis-à-vis enterprises with a more enlightened attitude.

More persuasively, one could argue that the number of hours one works is a rough index of overall attachment to the labor force, so that effort per hour will be positively correlated with hours of work. On this argument, the part-time labor force will supply less effort per hour than will full-timers and be paid less on that account. (For example, part-time work is relatively more common among older people, those with small children at home, and moonlighters, all of whom might be expected to have less effort to supply on the job.) If either of these arguments is correct, the low pay of part-timers overestimates the productivity loss that would occur if hours were reduced.

However, statistical evidence from the part-time labor market is consistent with the view that the net effect of a permanent reduction in working hours (to, say, thirty or thirty-five hours a week) on effort and efficiency impacts on effective labor input per hour would be strongly negative.[10] Such evidence should not be disregarded lightly.

QUALITY OF LABOR SUPPLY

There is some basis in neoclassical economic theory for a tentative prediction of a negative effect of hours reduction on the education and training, and hence in the long run on the skills, of the work force, although the argument is necessarily speculative. One might expect, first, a reduction in employer investment in on-the-job training. A rational employer response to a sharp cut in hours would be to redesign jobs where feasible, so that they were simpler and required less training. There is evidence that employers do redesign jobs when, due to changes in the quality of their local labor supply, they experience an increase in employee turnover and absenteeism. The same economic impetus for job simplification would be supplied by hours reduction.

In the longer run, a reduction in hours of work could also have negative effects on the schooling that the work force receives, and hence on its productivity. The crux of the argument is that a reduction in hours would reduce the financial rate of return to schooling, and so would tend to reduce investment in education. In the standard economic analysis of schooling as an investment in human capital, students and their families compare the earnings loss and other costs of an additional year of schooling with the financial and other benefits that are expected. The principal expected financial benefit is a higher hourly wage rate in the labor market; when the hourly wage rate gain is multiplied by total lifetime hours to be worked, an estimate is obtained of the expected financial return. By comparing this and other benefits of education with its costs, a family is able to make a rational decision on an additional year of schooling. A reduction in lifetime hours, through a sharp cut in weekly hours, would reduce the financial return to education, making further schooling less attractive. Some rough calculations indicate that a 25 percent reduction in weekly working hours will reduce the rate of return to education in about the same proportion—for example, from 8 percent to 6 percent.[11]

The expected effects of a change in the economic return to education on private and social investments in schooling are not as well established as are the effect of hours reduction on the return to schooling. Economic theory would predict that a reduction in working hours that substantially lowered the earnings return to schooling would, other things being equal, make expenditures for schooling less attractive and hence be expected to yield a somewhat lower investment in schooling—and, eventually, a less productive labor force.

Workweek reduction might have a similarly negative effect on that portion of the educational investment paid by school taxes. The economic return to society from education is reduced for the same reason that the private earnings return is cut. Moreover, the tax rate on earnings would have to be increased to pay for the present level of schooling, if earnings were reduced by a cut in hours. These two factors might induce taxpayers to cut back outlays for education. (Compare the discussion of the effects of hours reduction on public finances in chapter 13.)

Hours reduction could also have an important effect on the quality of education. Since the introduction of forty-eight- and then forty-hour work-weeks—along with vacations and holidays and earlier retirement—we have seen more concern with "education for life," relative to education for narrow career goals. Very likely, a reduction to a thirty- or thirty-two-hour workweek would further stimulate this trend. At least it is reasonable to speculate that a four-day workweek would yield more interest in courses that would prepare young people for the eighty to eighty-five waking hours a week not at work, possibly at the expense of those that prepared them for their thirty-two or so hours of paid work. Moreover, reductions in the working hours of adults could lead to reductions in the working hours of students and teachers, further weakening the investment in the productive skills of the work force.

Possible Offsets

Predictions of the effects of hours reduction on investment in the labor supply must be highly speculative. One cannot overemphasize the point that, while short-hours schedules in individual firms provide us with useful information for discussing the problems of fatigue and efficiency, we have no analogous empirical experience to forecast effects on education, which responds to many different forces in our society. For example, a shorter workweek would certainly make it much easier for working adults to continue their education. But it is very difficult to assess the importance of this point. While a thirty- or thirty-two-hour workweek would provide ample study time for the ambitious worker, the thirty-five- or forty-hour work-week also provides adequate time, yet most employees do not take advantage of this opportunity. The statistically average worker now puts in about twelve minutes a day in study. Moreover, of those workers who have tried evening study and abandoned it, only one in five report lack of time as a reason for dropping out. Hence, one can only guess at the likely magnitude of the effect of workweek reductions on adult education.

Here, too, the scenario method offers a way to reduce forecast error.[12] If hours are reduced as a rationing device (the second scenario) while most workers are eager to maintain their living standards, one might see a significant increase in career-oriented adult education as a form of disguised moonlighting. But if workers demand a shorter workweek simply because they want more time to spend with their families and in recreation (the first scenario), a much less positive effect should be expected.

Summary

In the long run, a reduction in the amount of labor supplied will be translated into a reduction in labor demanded or utilized. The effect of a reduction in scheduled hours per employed worker can be an equiproportional reduction in the amount of effective labor input utilized in market production; it can also be less than that, or possibly greater. The net effect is likely to be greatly influenced by the scenario or conditions in which the reduction takes place. If, in the first scenario, hours reduction is in conformance with increased demands for leisure time, one could well have a reduction in effective labor input at least equiproportionate to the reduction in hours. Offsets such as increased participation, moonlighting, and effort per hour would be minimized. More specifically, negative effects on the quality of labor supplied to the market in a leisure-oriented society could also result.[13]

In the second scenario, in which hours are reduced for social reasons despite individual preferences for the original schedule, one can more forcefully predict that an hours reduction policy will yield significantly less than proportionate reduction in effective labor input. Strong offsets are expected through increases in labor force participation, moonlighting, and worker effort on the job. And the quality of the labor force might even increase if workers used a portion of their enforced leisure to improve their skills through training and education.

CHAPTER TWELVE

National Output

THE LONG-RUN EFFECTS on national output of reducing the amount of labor utilized in production (by cutting hours per worker) depend in part upon the interaction of labor input with the nation's stock of plant, equipment, and other capital goods. These indirect effects of hours reduction can be extremely important, although they are most complicated and difficult to forecast. The interaction between hours of work and capital stock is somewhat different in the long run; in the short or medium run (considered in chapter 6), the effects of hours reduction on the use of the existing stock of capital goods are analyzed, while in the long-run analysis the effects of hours reduction on the supply of new machines through investment, and hence on the level of capital stock, are also important.

Domestic Capital Formation

Advocates of shorter hours have often argued that, if hours are reduced, capital will be substituted for labor at an accelerated pace, so that little long-term reduction in output should be expected. However, it is more likely that a reduction in capital investment, not an increase, will result from a decline in hours of work.

The labor replacement theory is essentially a generalization to the economy as a whole of experience at the firm or industry level. At the micro-level, when supply of labor is reduced, raising its relative price, capital is often substituted for labor, raising the capital-labor ratio in that sector.[1] But the financing for this investment in equipment comes out of total investment funds available in the economy. If these are fixed, increased investment in one sector simply means less investment elsewhere. Hence, trade union or government restrictions that lead to accelerated investment in a sector can be accomplished by a redistribution of funds. But if hours of work are reduced throughout the economy, there cannot be any compensatory increase in capital investment on an economywide basis if the total supply of investment funds is fixed. Capital investment would be increased only if funds are increased; if they are reduced, capital spending is reduced. Hence, one should restate the question of whether capital can be substituted for labor as one of whether the aggregate amount of investment funds is increased by a reduction in hours.

In most models, the domestic supply of funds for investment is based upon the supply of savings (personal or corporate). This is a function of profits and, to a lesser extent, labor earnings. But both types of income would be reduced by a reduction in hours of work. A decline in investment funds will, ceteris paribus, reduce capital stock.

It is difficult to predict the extent of the likely reduction in capital stock, since there are a number of competing models. But one can derive such predictions if one adopts some simplifying assumptions. In a simple model of economic growth, the rate of capital utilization is unaffected by hours reduction; investment is completely determined by domestic savings; savings is a function of profits and output; and capital stock is determined by past levels of investment. Then when hours of work are reduced, the capital-labor ratio is predicted at first to rise (because labor input is less), then to fall as capital stock is diminished (because output and hence savings and investment are lower). In a plausible variant of this model, the final result is that the capital-labor ratio is restored to its original level. (Examples of this are presented in the appendix to this chapter.)

This predicted effect of hours reduction has serious implications for our forecast of the impact on national output. If capital and labor are both reduced by the same proportion, a reasonable forecast would be a cut in output of about the same magnitude. For example, if a permanent reduction in hours of work from forty to thirty-two yielded a 25 percent net reduction in effective labor input, and if the long-term consequence was a reduction of capital stock by 25 percent from the level it would otherwise have reached, then it is plausible that national output would also be 25 percent below the level that could have been achieved with a forty-hour workweek.[2]

International Capital Flows

In practice, investment flows depend upon capital imports and exports, as well as upon domestic savings. Unfortunately, economists have paid very little attention to the effect of hours reduction on international capital flows. Alfred Marshall provided a notable exception, arguing that in the short run hours reduction would reduce profit margins (by reducing the amount of labor per unit of capital).[3] This would in turn induce capitalists to send their investable funds abroad, where the rate of return was higher. Marshall's analysis implies that as the capital-labor ratio is gradually reduced, through lower levels of investment at home, profit margins would gradually be restored, eventually eliminating the incentive to invest abroad. The final equilibrium is identical to that obtained if international capital flows are ignored: the original capital-labor ratio is also restored. The difference between the two assumptions is that capital stock declines more rapidly toward equilibrium if we allow for the export of profits (since not only are profits reduced by a cut in hours, but a smaller proportion of them is reinvested in home industries during the transition period).[4]

In practice, though, the possibility of international flows of capital requires a still more complicated analysis. In the first place, there are obstacles to the international movement of capital because of the preferences companies and individual savers have for investing in their own countries and because of institutional factors. This permits differences in rates of return among countries to persist and so would moderate the decline in capital stock resulting from hours reduction.

A more serious objection to this assessment is that it implicitly assumes that each country offers the same production opportunities. This would make sense if each country's economy consisted simply of an abstract combination of capital and labor. It would then be reasonable to argue that if capital is free to move across international boundaries, and if the labor supply is reduced in one country, capital will (barring institutional or cultural obstacles) likely be exported to where labor is relatively abundant.

But the productive resources of each nation are diverse. They have special endowments—land, materials, and energy, for example—and these complicate our analysis. An extreme example illustrates the point: if, at a time when world petroleum stocks are low, the workweek in oil-rich Kuwait or Abu Dhabi were cut by one-fourth, who would doubt that labor-saving machinery would be rushed into those nations in order to maintain oil output? While the United States is not Abu Dhabi, and is in close competition for investment funds with other advanced industrialized nations, it does have important immobile resources, such as land and minerals, and their economic value would reduce any tendency to export capital.

This point has generally been ignored by economists in the discussion of work time reduction. But it can be shown that the net effect of hours reduction upon capital exports depends upon whether a reduction in labor inputs increases or decreases the marginal productivity of capital. If there are just two factors, capital and labor, it is likely that the productivity of capital will vary positively with the amount of labor available to utilize it. But if capital and labor are working with another input or set of inputs, the productivity of capital could conceivably be increased by a reduction in labor input—as in the hypothetical case of an oil-producing state. A formal economic analysis predicts that the outcome depends on whether there are better substitution possibilities between capital and labor or between variable factors (capital and labor together) on the one hand and fixed factors (land, water, minerals, climate, and so on) on the other, and also on the relative importance of fixed factors. Only if fixed factors are quite important, and the possibilities of substitution between variable and fixed factors small relative to the possibility of substituting capital for labor, will the productivity of capital increase.

In the United States, with its very large and highly skilled labor force and its extensive capital stock, it is unlikely that a reduction in labor would increase the productivity of capital or produce net capital imports. However, the extensive natural resources of our country would be expected to yield some partial restraint on the export of capital, which one would otherwise expect if hours were reduced.

Capital Utilization in the Long Run

The analysis so far has concluded that a plausible long-term consequence of a reduction in hours would be a decline in both capital stock and output in roughly the same proportion as the drop in labor input.[5] But an even more pessimistic conclusion is indicated if the negative effects of workweek reduction on the utilization of capital are taken into account.

It has been estimated that in normally prosperous times, machinery in the United States is used about 30 percent of the time. This can be achieved with a forty-hour standard workweek, plus about three to four hours a week of overtime, and the employment of an average of one evening or night worker for every eight day workers. A 25 percent reduction in working hours would, other things being equal (i.e., with the same overtime and shift work ratios), reduce the utilization rate by the same proportion—from about three-tenths to about two-ninths.[6]

The utilization rate has implications for the long-term supply of capital. (These are worked out in a less informal way in the appendix to this chapter.) Assume that in the long run labor and capital are fully employed. Assume also (for the moment) that only a single shift is worked. Then the number of machines or work stations must equal the number of workers. Any long-term changes in the capital-labor ratio must then necessarily take the form of a change in capital investment per machine. It follows that the reduction in capital stock predicted as a long-term consequence of a cut in hours would result in each worker having less capital invested in the machine or work station at which he is employed. In the simple example used above, in which a 25 percent reduction in hours per worker yielded a 25 percent reduction in capital stock, one would have 25 percent less capital invested in each machine. In this case, the capital-labor ratio— in the sense of the ratio of capital stock to hours worked—is unchanged. But in a more meaningful sense—the amount of capital per *employee*—the capital-labor ratio is reduced. Taking into account this effect—the reduction in what might be called the *effective* capital-labor ratio—yields a prediction of a more than proportionate reduction in output.

The long-term analysis can also be modified to take into account any lengthening of the useful life of machinery due to lower utilization, and a consequently lower rate of physical depreciation. Several writers have argued that this adjustment is small, because in many industries obsolescence due to technical change is a more important factor than physical depreciation and because idle machinery can sometimes deteriorate as rapidly as that in use. Nevertheless, this adjustment does moderate the predicted negative result, although it does not change the fact that a somewhat more than proportionate reduction in output will be obtained with a reduction in hours of work.[7]

Effects of an Increase in Shift Work

The negative effects on capital intensity may also be moderated if shift work is increased. The short-run production gains from increasing shift work in a fully employed economy are quite limited (compare the discussion in chapter 6). When hours are reduced with full employment, there are, by assumption, no additional workers to put on shifts. Moreover, capital stock is fixed in the short run. But in the long run, plant construction decisions can be made that exploit expected increases in the proportion of shift workers.

To see this, consider the influence of shift work on the number of machines or work stations that must be available to maintain full employment. In practice, full employment of labor requires only that there be enough machines to employ the largest shift (presumably the day shift). Hence, as the proportion on other shifts is increased (and the proportion on day shifts reduced), the number of machines needed declines. If we continue to assume that total investment is constant, a smaller number of machines to be constructed means that employers can invest more capital per machine. In fact, it can be shown that, if shift work is increased to the point that there is no reduction in the rate of capacity utilization when hours are reduced (i.e., to the point where the hours that each machine works are maintained at the old level), no net reduction in capital per worker need ensue, and output need fall only in proportion to the decline in hours worked.[8] These points can perhaps be seen more clearly with the help of a simple example. (The reader not interested in this example can skip directly to Prospects for Shift Work.)

An Example of the Effects on Capital Utilization

In this example, let H equal the number of hours per worker; P the proportion of workers on alternative shifts (and $1 - P$ the proportion on day shifts); and H^* the maximum number of hours a machine can be used per week. Then, if there are n workers, $n(1 - P)$ will be employed on the day shift. If the day shift is the largest shift, $n(1 - P)$ machines must be available to avoid unemployment of labor.

Given full employment of labor, total use of the machines (on all shifts) will equal nH working hours per week. Capacity usage of machines will equal the number of machines times the maximum number of hours each machine can be used, or $n(1 - P)H^*$. Hence, the utilization rate will equal the ratio of usage to capacity, or

$$U = nH/[n(1 - P)H^*] = H/[H^*(1 - P)].$$

In principle, then, an increase in P, the night shift proportion, can offset a reduction in hours, leaving utilization unchanged. This will occur if the proportion of day workers, $1 - P$, declines at the same rate as the hours per shift, H.

Table 12.1 gives a numerical example of the utilization problem. Initially, each worker is employed 44 hours a week (including overtime). Since one-ninth of the work is on the night shift, each machine is utilized about 49.5 hours a week (scenario A). If maximum feasible utilization, H^*, is 150 hours a week, the utilization rate, U, is about one-third. If employment equals 100 million workers, 88.9 million machines, or work stations, are required: $n(1 - P)$. Now let hours be reduced by 25 percent, without a change in the shiftwork ratio (scenario B). Utilization will then decline in the same proportion (to about 37.1 hours, or one-fourth of capacity). But if shift work triples when hours are reduced (scenario C), utilization is maintained at the original level of one-third of capacity (49.5 hours per week).

A Hypothetical Example of the Effects on Output

The economic effect of such a compensatory change in utilization can be explicated with a further extension of the numerical example in table 12.1. Using some hypothetical numbers for the relation between output and input yields an output of $1,018 billion as long-term equilibrium level of output, and $4.63 as the long-term level of output per hour worked.[9] Total capital stock of $2,035 billion is generated, while capital per machine or work station is $22,861. When hours are reduced without an increase in shift work, capital per work station drops, and output per hour drops by 7

TABLE 12.1. Long-Term Effects of Hours Reduction:
A Hypothetical Example

Item	Scenarios		
	A	B	C
Standard hours per worker	40	30	30
Total hours per worker	44	33	33
Proportion of labor force on night shift	1/9	1/9	1/3
Utilization			
hours per week	49.5	37.1	49.5
proportion of maximum	1/3	1/4	1/3
machines or work stations (millions)	88.9	88.9	66.7
output per year (millions of dollars)	1,018	694	763
output per hour (dollars)	4.63	4.20	4.63
capital stock (billions of dollars)	2,035	1,367	1,527
capital stock per machine or work station (dollars)	22,864	15,602	22,864

percent as a result. This yields a total drop in output of 32 percent (a 25 percent reduction in hours and a 7 percent reduction in output per hour).

But when hours reduction is accompanied by an increase in the shift-work ratio, the number of machines needed for full employment is reduced by a quarter, to 66.7 million. As a result, while total capital stock also declines by one-fourth, no reduction is imposed on capital per machine. Similarly, output is reduced by 25 percent, but since this reduction is induced by a 25 percent cut in hours, output per hour remains constant.

Of course, this hypothetical example abstracts from many real work problems. Expected trends in population growth, labor force participation, and technical advances also influence long-term investment decisions. In a growing, technically progressive economy, one is more likely to observe a slowing down of the process of substituting capital for labor and a lower rate of growth of the labor supply, rather than reversals of these trends, as a result of a shorter workweek. Nevertheless, one would expect the net effects of a reduction in hours of work or of an increase in shift work to be in the direction predicted by the simpler economic analysis.

Prospects for Shift Work

It is easier to design an economic model to predict the expected effects of an increase in shift work resulting from a reduction in hours than to predict the extent to which shift work will actually respond to hours reduction. The scenario approach is of some assistance here. If hours are reduced by statute, for social reasons, despite the continued preferences by individuals for income over leisure (as in the second scenario), theory predicts that it would likely be relatively easy to recruit shift workers if a reasonable premium were paid. But if hours are reduced simply because of a decline in the work ethic—expressed in an increased reluctance of workers to give up time spent with their families or in recreational pursuits—it is reasonable to expect a similar reluctance to work shifts that interfere with family life, recreation pursuits, and so on. The best hope of the employer in this first scenario for hours reduction is that the preference for increased leisure will not be universal, so that some workers will be seeking ways to supplement income.

The past association of shift work and hours reduction may be instructive here. Available data show a clear pattern of increases in shift work in the United States from at least the 1920s. About one in nine of all those employed as wage and salary workers in the nonagricultural sector work on nonstandard shifts, while almost three out of ten production workers in manufacturing are on evening or night shifts.[10] British and European data show a similarly sharp increase since the 1950s. This upward trend at first appears difficult to explain: it seems to run counter to changes in work schedules that give the employee more freedom—shorter full-time schedules, the growth of the part-time market, and the development of compressed workweeks and flexitime. But several factors have fostered the growth of shift work.

On the employer demand side, workweek reduction probably has been a factor in increased use of shift workers. The standard workweek in this country was reduced from forty-eight to forty hours in the 1930s and 1940s. In a number of European countries, this reduction was carried out in the fifties and sixties. This correlation would be consistent with the view that workweek reduction has increased the demand for shift workers. Some evidence in favor of this hypothesis is presented by Murray Foss, who found that those industries with the longest weekly hours schedules in 1929 had the largest increases in shift work in the ensuing years.[11] This could be rationalized by arguing that employers had a need to maintain capital utilization or that employees were less resistant to shift work when the workweek was lower.

Other factors also increased employer demand. It has been argued that an acceleration in the rate of technical progress has increased the importance of obsolescence of plant (relative to its physical depreciation) as a determinant of the effective life of capital stock. The economic analysis of shift work would imply that a change in this direction would help to tip the scales in favor of greater use of shifts by employers. (Increased shift work would increase the rate of physical depreciation but allow the employer to obtain profits from the plant within a shorter period of time.) Other demand side explanations emphasize technical developments in industries that use shift work, expansion of the health care and protection industries which utilize shifts, and longer hours of operation for many retail trade and service establishments.

On the employee or supply side, the greater amenities available to shift workers today are cited as an explanation of the continued acceptance of nonstandard schedules. At low per capita income, workers must live in noisy, overcrowded dwellings, and this makes it difficult for them to sleep during the day. Similarly, a lack of electricity limits their enjoyment of nighttime leisure. According to this argument, a lack of such amenities was an important deterrent to shift working until quite recent times and helps to explain the comparatively low level of shift work found in developing nations. High wage rates and smaller families have increased per capita income in the United States, enabling shift workers to ease the discomfort imposed by their schedules. (The relation between amenities and shift work is discussed further in chapter 14.)

This variety of explanations makes it most difficult to ascertain the extent to which workweek reduction was responsible for past increases in shift work or to forecast just how large an increase in shift work would be elicited by a further reduction in work time. There are, moreover, further complicating circumstances:

1. If shift work is to be increased on a large scale, it will be necessary to involve individuals whose personality, sex, age, family responsibilities, or other circumstances have made them heretofore reluctant to accept alternative shifts. It is difficult to predict whether even a sharp increase in the premium paid for shift work would be sufficient to induce them to change their behavior.

2. The extent to which shift work will respond to hours reduction depends on the type of reduction. Extended vacations with only a small reduction in the workweek might have little effect. On the other hand, a sharply reduced workweek could permit a number of alternative shifts. For

example, two six-hour-a-day shifts, back to back (say 6 A.M. to noon and noon to 6 P.M.), could extend the workday of machinery without causing very serious discomfort to workers on either shift. (Compare the discussion in chapter 14.)

3. Recent research has focused attention on the physical and mental health costs imposed on shift workers, and there are some who would ban shift work altogether (at least where shifts are worked for profit, rather than to provide for community emergencies or for some other social goal). It is not unlikely that shift work will be subject to more government regulation in the years ahead.[12]

4. The nature and level of amenities to be provided to shift workers in the years ahead is unknown.

Perhaps the most plausible forecast that one can make in the face of all this uncertainty is that the effect of a reduction in hours is most likely to be some reduction in capital utilization along with some increase in shift work. Very likely, those sectors that now make the heaviest use of shift work will continue to do so. Indeed, where capital costs are very high, economic pressure may justify paying whatever shift work premia are necessary to maintain utilization at the present level. But in other industries, a relatively sharp cutback in utilization would be more likely. At the aggregate level, this forecast would imply reductions in output over and beyond those resulting when capital utilization is maintained.[13]

Conclusions

1. A reduction in labor supplied to the market will in the long run mean a reduction in labor utilized in the economy, not a reduction in unemployment.

2. The effects of a reduction in hours of work on national output very much depends on whether it reflects the income-leisure preferences of the work force or whether it occurs in opposition to these preferences, through government legislation or other collective agreements designed to serve social goals.

3. If work time reduction does reflect increased demand for leisure, the effects on national output will be large. It may mean an equiproportionate reduction in effective labor supply, as the diseconomies of short-hours schedules come to outweigh any offsets through increased labor force participation or other compensating gains in labor supply. And a reduction in labor supply may then mean at least a proportionate reduction in capital

stock. This effect will be exacerbated if increased demand for leisure time for family and recreation activities coincides with a resistance to shift work. There may also be negative long-term effects on training and schooling, as the force of market incentives is weakened. Hence, a reduction in work time in this scenario could mean an equiproportionate reduction in output as well as in effective labor supply: for example, a reduction of the workweek from forty to thirty-two hours could lower national output 25 percent below what it otherwise would be.

4. On the other hand, if hours reduction is introduced as a social policy, the effect on national output will be much less. A combination of shorter schedules—with fewer hours to spend on the job and more hours off the job—and a widespread interest in replacing income lost as a result of the work time restriction would be expected to yield a number of positive offsets to the initial production loss: greater effort on the job, especially where productivity bargaining is used; a sharp increase in moonlighting; increased participation in the full-time labor market by women, older males, and students; and greater acceptance of shift work. Participation in schooling and training for marketable occupations would also be enhanced. These positive offsets would probably be greater if work time reduction took the form of a shorter workday rather than of increased vacation and holiday time. For example, if the dominant schedule became a six-hour workday, five-day workweek, one could have:

- Exploitation of the gain in effort per hour made possible by a six-hour day.
- Moonlighters putting in two sequential shifts, without serious sleep disturbance. For example, a 6 A.M. to 12 P.M. shift in one establishment could be complemented with a 12:30 P.M. to 6:30 P.M. shift in another. This could increase further the rate of moonlighting.
- Couples using sequential shifts (with one spouse working in the mornings, the other in the afternoons) so as to maximize the time that children would be supervised by parents. This could permit still greater participation in the full-time labor market by mothers of young children.
- Older workers postponing retirement.
- Establishments able to maintain or even extend the workday of machinery by using shifts.

Thus, if work time is reduced for social reasons—perhaps on the (very likely mistaken) grounds that this is necessary to avoid large-scale unemployment—the long-term cost in national output forgone will be much less than if work time is reduced because of a genuine desire for more leisure.

Appendix to Chapter Twelve

A. THE SIMPLE CASE

If output (O) is a linear homogenous function of labor and capital,

$$O = f(C, nH), \tag{1}$$

where O_{nH}, O_C, O_{CnH} are greater than zero, and O_{nHnH}, O_{CC} are less than zero. Then rewriting equation (1) in terms of output per man-hour, we obtain

$$O/nH = f(C/nH). \tag{2}$$

Let C/O be proportionate to I/O in the long run; then

$$C/O = mI/0. \tag{3}$$

This implies that the effect on C/O and C/nH of a change in H depends upon the effect of the change on I/O. Savings and investment in a closed economy might be assumed in a simple model to be proportionate to output or, alternatively, to the income received by capital (assumed equal to the product of the marginal product of capital and capital stock); that is, to either

$$I/O = w, \tag{4a}$$

or

$$I/O = O_C Cx, \tag{4b}$$

where w and x are constants. In equation (4a), we can write, using equations (2), (3), and (4a),

$$O/nH = f(mwO/nH). \tag{5}$$

This implies (making the usual assumptions about the differentiability of O)

$$E_{O,H} = 1 + E_{f,C/nH}(E_{O,H} - 1) = 1, \tag{6}$$

where E denotes elasticity (and $E_{f,(C/nH)} \neq 1$). In equation (4b), using equations (2), (3), and (4b),

$$C/mO = (C/O)O_C x, \tag{7}$$

so

$$O_C = m/x. \tag{8}$$

Since O_C is a single valued function of C/nH, equation (8) implies by the linear homogeneity assumption that C/nH, and hence $f(C/nH)$, are constant. So

$$E_{O,H} = 1. \tag{9}$$

B. International Capital Flows

Let output be determined by a third factor of production, M, representing fixed supplies of materials, energy, and so on, in addition to labor and capital.

$$O = O(L, C, M). \tag{10}$$

In the two-factor case, it was reasonable to assume that the marginal product of capital would decline with a reduction in labor input; that is, that O_{CL} was positive. But this is not so plausible an implication in the three-factor case. It is interesting here to consider production as a two-stage process, in which labor, L, and capital, C, are combined to produce a manmade input, I, which is then combined with a natural resource, M, to yield output, O. If

$$I = I(L, C), \tag{11}$$

$$O = O(M, I), \tag{12}$$

then

$$\partial O/\partial C = O_I I_C, \tag{13}$$

and

$$\partial^2 O/\partial C \partial L = O_I I_{CL} + I_C O_{LL} I_L. \tag{14}$$

If equations (11) and (12) are linear homogenous functions, equation (14) can be rewritten as

$$\partial^2 O/\partial C \partial L = [O_I I_C I_L/I] [1/s_{LC} - R_M/s_{IM}], \tag{15}$$

where s_{LC} is the elasticity of substitution between L and C, and $R_M = (MO_M/O) s_{IM}$ is the elasticity of substitution between I and M. Equation (15) can be rewritten more concisely in elasticity form as

$$E_{\partial O/\partial C, L} = R_L[(1/s_{LC}) - (R_M/s_{IM})]. \tag{16}$$

Here, the marginal product of capital will be increased by a cutback in hours (the Abu Dhabi case) if and only if R_M exceeds s_{IM}/s_{LC}.

C. THE UTILIZATION PROBLEM

The model can also be modified to take into account the effects of variations in the utilization of capital. If one ignores these issues (as we have to this point), variations in the size of the labor force and in the number of hours per worker are treated symmetrically. However, the two dimensions of labor supply have asymmetric effects upon utilization and hence on output. To see this, assume that the labor force, n, and capital stock, C, are fully employed in equilibrium. Let the number of workers on night shifts equal Pn and the number on day shifts equal $(1 - P)n$; let $(1 - P)n$ exceed Pn. Then $(1 - P)n$ machines are required for full employment of labor, and $C/(1 - P)n$ capital per machine is required for the full employment of capital. Ignoring for now any relation between depreciation and utilization, it can be argued that the correct measure of the capital-labor ratio is capital per machine. Using this measure, rewrite equation (2) as

$$O/nH = f[C/n(1 - P)], \tag{17}$$

with O a linear homogenous function of n and C. In the short run (i.e., holding C constant), equation (2) would imply

$$E_{O,H} = 1 - E_{f,H}, \tag{18}$$

or using the linear homogeneity property,

$$E_{O,H} = R_n, \tag{19}$$

where $R_n = nO_n/O$. But in the model in which utilization is explicitly considered (equation 17), we obtain, in the short run,

$$E_{O,H} = 1. \tag{20}$$

In the long run, C varies. If equation (3) holds, then using equation (4a) first, we obtain

$$O/nH = f[mwO/n(1 - P)] \tag{21}$$

and

$$E_{O,H} = 1 + E_{f(C/nH)} E_{O,H} \tag{22}$$

or

$$E_{O,H} = 1/R_n = 1 + (1 - R_n)/R_n. \tag{23}$$

In the (4b) variant, equation (8) continues to hold, but the definition of f has changed. Now, from equation (17),

$$O_C = (f'nH)/[n(1 - P)] = f'H/(1 - P) \tag{24}$$

and, combining equations (8) and (24),

$$f' = \{[m(1 - P)]/x\}1/H. \tag{25}$$

Differentiating both sides of equation (25) w.r.t. C and H yields

$$[f''/n^2(1 - P)^2]dC = - (m/xnH^2)dH, \tag{26}$$

or

$$E_{C,H} = -1/E_{f'.C/n(1-P)}. \tag{27}$$

If equation (1) can be approximated by a constant elasticity of substitution form, it follows that

$$E_{f'.C/n(1-P)} = -R_n/s, \tag{28}$$

where s is the elasticity of substitution between capital and labor. Substituting equation (28) in equation (27) yields

$$E_{C,H} = s/R_n. \tag{29}$$

In the long run, equation (17) implies

$$E_{O,H} = 1 + (1 - R_n)E_{C,H}. \tag{30}$$

Or, using equation (29),

$$E_{O,H} = 1 + [(1 - R_n)/R_n]^s. \tag{31}$$

If $s = 1$, this will yield the same result as was obtained when I/O was assumed to have a constant equilibrium value; see equation (23).

D. Depreciation

Depreciation can be increased by utilization. Let D equal annual depreciation of the capital stock, and i, investment net of depreciation:

$$i = I - D. \tag{32}$$

Then

$$v = i/I = 1 - D/I \tag{33}$$

affords a measure of the relative importance of depreciation. The effects of H on v can readily be incorporated into our model. Equation (3) is replaced with

$$C/O = m(i/O) = mv(I/O). \tag{34}$$

If we make the assumption that gross investment is *not* increased as a result of higher depreciation but is entirely borne as a reduction in i, then, in the model in which gross investment is proportionate to output, equation (4a),

$$C/O = wvm \tag{35}$$

should then be rewritten as

$$O/nH = f[mvwO/n(1 - P)], \tag{36}$$

yielding

$$E_{O,H} = 1 + (1 - R_n)(E_{O,H} + E_{v,H}), \tag{37}$$

or

$$E_{O,H} = 1 + [(1 - R_n)/Rn] (1 + E_{v,H}). \tag{38}$$

If the model in equation (4b) is used instead, we have—again using equation (34)—

$$O_C = 1/mvx. \tag{39}$$

From equations (39) and (24) we obtain

$$1/mvx = (1 + f')/1 - P. \tag{40}$$

Differentiating equation (40) and calculating elasticities yields

$$-E_{v,H} = 1 + E_{f',C/n(1-P)}E_{C,H}, \tag{41}$$

or

$$E_{C,H} = (1 + E_{v,H})/E_{f',C/n(1-P)}. \tag{42}$$

Again using the approximations for $E_{f'} [C/n(1 - P)]$ in equation (28), we obtain

$$E_{C,H} = (1 + E_{v,H})s/R_n. \tag{43}$$

Similarly, from equation (30),

$$E_{O,H} = 1 - (1 + E_{v,H})/E_{f',C/n(1-P)}. \tag{44}$$

Or, using the CES approximation,

$$E_{O,H} = 1 + [(1 - R_n)/R_n] s(1 + E_{v,H}). \tag{45}$$

Again, the result obtained when $s = 1$ is identical to that found in the model when equation (4a) is used; compare equation (38). These results show that depreciation will reduce the importance of utilization to some extent; they also indicate that, as long as utilization increases, the net investment rate, $E_{O,H}$, will exceed unity.[14]

CHAPTER THIRTEEN

Social and Economic Consequences

A MAJOR, permanent reduction in work time that also reduced economic output would have profound social as well as economic consequences. Some notion of its likely impact can be obtained by looking at former reductions. Consider, for example, the truly vast changes made possible in the United States in the past fifty years as a result of the movement from a six-day to a five-day workweek and the introduction of annual vacations for most employees.

The discussion in this chapter is limited to those expected effects with an obvious and direct relation to the predicted impacts on work time and income. Other effects are also likely, though more difficult to predict. For example, a reduction in work time might well lead to a more equal distribution of power and of household chores between men and women. This is expected to be a more likely result if work time reduction takes the form of a shorter workday rather than, say, longer vacations. (This point has been stressed by some Swedish feminists.[1]) Important effects on education are also likely (in addition to the output effects discussed in chapter 11). For example, if work time reduction takes place, but time spent in school is not changed, the number of hours spent in school would begin to approximate the hours spent in the workplace. But this raises the possibility of synchronizing schedules: it might require only that the schoolday be extended an hour or so and that summer vacation be shortened. Such synchronization of school and workplace would have wide implications for the problem of child care.

These are only some of the interesting effects of a much reduced work time. But while eschewing such difficult-to-analyze effects, the following discussion addresses specific implications of a change in work time and income for five social or economic impact areas: government finances; materials and energy problems; leisure; recreation; and metropolitan growth.

Government Finances

If hours reduction yields a long-term decline in output, then there are just two possible results for public finances: expenditures must be cut or tax rates must be raised (assuming that we do not increase national debt still further). Of course, if hours are cut in a high-growth scenario, this prediction is modified: the growth rate in federal expenditure has to be lower than it otherwise would be, or taxes must be raised. With weak growth, an absolute decline in federal revenues is more likely.

Pressure on government finances is also moderated insofar as some important government programs are directly or indirectly linked to the rate of growth in per capita income. According to this argument, if work time reduction slows down or reverses economic growth, the rate of government spending required is also reduced. There is some merit to this view: a major portion of federal outlays is allocated to welfare and Social Security payments, and a historical analysis of welfare programs shows that the American commitment to the poor—or at least its concept of the poverty line or of the appropriate social minimum wage—rises along with growth in per capita income. Moreover, Social Security and other retirement plans have been concerned with providing protection against income decline in old age, not simply an absolute income floor. In fact, present Social Security regulations require that pension benefits be based upon earlier earnings. In addition, outlays designed to service business and consumers (e.g., the postal service) might be expected to decline with a lower material living standard.

However, this offset does not mean that hours reduction poses no difficulties for public finances. While aid to the poor and the elderly may in the long run adjust to new income levels, that run can be rather long indeed. The Congress does have the power to reduce Social Security benefits, but it is very reluctant to use it and may well regard the cuts in retirement benefits required by hours reduction as undesirable, both socially and politically. Similarly, a sharp reduction in welfare, food stamps, disability payments, Medicaid, and other subsidies to the poor may also be socially and politically unacceptable.

Moreover, much of the budget is not affected at all by hours reduction. After Social Security, the largest expenditures are for defense, and outlays for this purpose are presumably determined in an international dialectic of forces, at least partly beyond the control of the national government. A significant reduction in output might force a hard choice between higher taxes for this purpose and a reevaluation of political and military commitments. Hence, the most likely effects of hours reduction in the low-growth scenario is some increase in tax rates, accompanied by some decline in government spending. In a high-growth scenario, a slowdown in growth of resources available for government programs is the more likely outcome.

All the fiscal effects mentioned above result from the impact of hours reduction on income. But there are other fiscal effects that are direct results of changes in work time. Possible effects on government spending on education programs were noted in chapter 11. The impact on metropolitan growth (see below) predicts that hours reduction could stimulate an outward movement of people and jobs, and this would require additional public funds for the construction and maintenance of metropolitan area social infrastructures. Similarly, increased requirements for funds for public recreation facilities, especially parks, are indicated in the analysis of recreation (below). These few examples indicate that social adjustments necessitated by a reduction in hours—with a consequent increase in time off—would impose new fiscal demands upon the state.

Materials and Energy Management

The experience of the energy crises of the 1970s taught economists to put more emphasis on materials and energy as essential factors of production, along with capital and labor. The effects of hours reductions on materials and energy problems are, however, quite complex and require a further extension of the usual analysis. Some writers try to simplify the argument; they begin by observing that layoffs result when oil or coal supplies are cut off. It is an easy (if misguided) step to the conclusion that a four-day workweek for all would be a rational, fair, long-term method of dealing with energy or material shortages, on the grounds that if less employment had to be provided, less materials and energy would be needed, even in the long run.

This is an oversimplification, since a reduction in working hours could damage as well as improve long-term prospects for dealing with materials and energy problems. It is true that a reduction in labor input would, if factor proportions remained unchanged, lead to less materials and energy usage. But empirical work indicates that there are considerable substitution possibilities between labor on the one hand and materials and energy on the other. And while economic growth in past decades was stimulated by the development of myriad devices fostering substitution of mineral energy for human labor, energy conservation now appears to require that this trend be slowed down.

Once this possibility is admitted, a number of implications follow for the discussion of hours reduction.[2] For example, two ways of dealing with the energy and materials constraint are conservation of demand and expansion of supplies. But a reduction in hours of work may make it more difficult to maintain popular support for a policy of energy conservation through reductions in the amount of energy used per worker (or at least through minimizing increases). Conservation policy and hours reduction policy both tend to reduce the material standard of living of workers. If this standard is being reduced by hours reduction, one might see resistance to further reductions as a result of conservation measures.

Moreover, hours reduction will also make it more difficult to increase the available supply of energy and materials. These can be increased either by using low-grade deposits or by developing new sources of supply. But the use of low-grade deposits requires much more labor per unit of energy or material secured, while a large-scale input of technical labor will be needed to develop alternative supply sources. A reduction in the amount of labor available will make it more difficult to achieve such goals.[3]

Leisure Time

It may seem redundant to seek to determine the effect of a reduction in hours of work on leisure time. After all, if we are talking about a real reduction in hours worked—not one offset by a decline in unemployment or by increased overtime, moonlighting, and labor force participation—a superficial judgment would be that a decline in hours of work would have to increase leisure time. But that result need not follow. Data on the ways in which Americans spend their time each week indicate that time not spent at paid employment is often spent at work or quasi-work activities: commuting, housework, child care, and so on. Hence, it is conceivable that a decline in hours of paid work would yield such a sharp increase in household production time that leisure time would not increase at all.

This is not a likely result in the scenario in which a gradual reduction in hours results from increased demands for time off as hourly wages rise (the first scenario). That scenario probably would be accompanied by an increase in leisure. My own rough calculations suggest that, on the basis of past experience, the most plausible result would be that the increase in time off would be divided in roughly the same proportions as the present leisure-household production mix (so that if 60 percent is now devoted to household production time, a ten-hour reduction in market employment time would yield a gain of six hours in household production time and four hours in consumption time).[4]

There is no guarantee that the future will repeat the past, especially since this scenario forecasts increases in both time and goods to unprecedented levels of general affluence—one certainly cannot rule out a change in the future division between leisure and other time. But it does seem implausible that *no* increase in leisure time would result from a decline in working hours that was a product of an increased preference for time off.

A DIFFERENT VIEW: THE LINDER ARGUMENT

A different view was expressed in *The Harried Leisure Class,* an influential book analyzing the allocation of time between leisure and household production.[5] Staffen Linder argued that growth in leisure time has been constrained, despite reduction in the workweek, because Americans have been condemned to spend large amounts of time in household production in order to service their extraordinarily high level of living. When one considers the average American family, with myriad appliances to maintain, large wardrobes, and high standards of personal cleanliness, but with a dearth of servants, it is easy to accept the view that it has less free time than similarly rich families enjoyed in earlier generations.

Linder's analysis is somewhat one-sided, however, as a characterization of changes over time in the leisure of the *average* American. Economic development has also produced a variety of timesavers in the home—from vacuum cleaners to fast foods—and has given Americans the income to purchase them. These effects of development would in themselves tend to reduce household production time, especially for the average citizen (who has never been able to afford servants). And, in fact, the available data, which show very little change over time in the distribution of time between leisure and household production, indicate that the various influences on this distribution are offsetting.

ENFORCED HOURS REDUCTION

A forecast of leisure time effects is more difficult in the second scenario, when hours are reduced by law with no accompanying change in the willingness of workers to sacrifice material living standards for increased leisure.[6] In this scenario, living standards could be at least partly protected by substituting household production time for market production. Since do-it-yourself is a notoriously inefficient substitute for market services, more rather than less total work time would be required if living standards were to be fully maintained. Some workers might seek to do most home repair and improvement themselves, maintain their own clothes, or even grow a portion of their own food. In the long run, they might gravitate to less expensive residences, where land was cheaper. The substitution of household production time for market work time would also include the use of slower, cheaper transportation modes—for example, taking buses rather than private cars.[7]

In summary, the intuitive judgment that a decline in working hours will yield an increase in leisure time for the average employee is probably correct. But this tendency will be much stronger if hours are reduced as a result of individual preferences, expressed in the market, than if the reduction comes as a result of policy designed to further social ends.

THE TREND TOWARD LARGER LEISURE MODULES

There has been a long-term trend toward taking time off in the form of longer periods, or modules. Up to the late 1920s, almost all of the progress made in reducing hours was in shortening the workday: the six-day workweek with no vacations remained the standard. This early form of hours reduction made sense because of the relatively harmful effects on health, productivity, and family life of a long workday.

But with the establishment of an eight- or nine-hour workday, an increasing number of firms introduced a five-day workweek. By the end of the 1930s, the five-day workweek became the norm in much of manufacturing, and by the 1960s, the five-day schedule had been almost universally adopted in nonagricultural industries. The postwar era also saw the extension of annual vacations to blue collar workers and an increase in annual holidays.

There is pressure to continue this trend: when polled, Americans state a strong preference for taking additional time off in the form of vacations and holidays rather than as a shorter workday.[8] Moreover, it is not hard to understand this employee preference. A reduction in the number of workdays reduces the number of commuting trips. An increase in the size of the leisure time module also provides economies of scale in leisure activities. Even a one-day holiday permits workers to enjoy the daylight hours, while longer modules permits more ambitious trips and excursions.

Nevertheless, it is not certain that the trend will continue. It was noted in the previous chapter that there may be greater opportunities for reducing the economic cost of work time reduction if it takes the form of a shorter workday. (At least in the second scenario, where the probability is higher of workers cooperating with managers in fitting their schedules to employers' needs.) If these economic considerations dominate, a reversal of the trend toward larger leisure modules is plausible.

Recreational Spending

The projected effects of hours reduction on recreational or leisure spending are (unlike the effects on leisure time) counterintuitive: past experience would forecast a net decline in recreational spending.

Studies have shown that recreational spending is closely linked to variations in income. Over 90 percent of the variation over time in per capita recreational consumption can be explained by just two variables—income and the price of recreation. Moreover, cross-sectional data on recreational spending at different income levels indicate a similarly positive relation. Both data sources show that for every 1 percent increase in income, outlays for recreation rise by about 1 percent or more, so that the share of recreation in income increases. On the other hand, changes in the amount of leisure time appear to have little effect on recreational outlays.[9] For example, the share of consumption allocated to recreation did not change much in the 1930s, when the workweek dropped sharply. On the other hand, it rose from 1948 to 1969, when income rose but hours of work showed little net change.

The explanation of the relation between recreational spending and income (rather than leisure) is clear enough: the remarkable ability of consumers to move to ever more expensive recreational pursuits as their income increases, even if their leisure hours remain unchanged. It is possible that a lack of leisure did constrain leisure spending in an earlier era: when the workweek for many employees was sixty or seventy hours per week and vacations were rare, additional free time very likely was essential for the development of a mass recreational market. However, the free time available with an eight-hour workday, five-day workweek, and with nine or ten annual holidays and a two-week vacation, apparently provides more than enough scope for a continuous rise in recreational spending.[10]

If recreational spending is sensitive to income changes rather than to changes in leisure, and if a reduction in hours reduces spendable income, then one would predict that a reduction in work time will reduce recreational spending. Of course, in the high-growth scenario, the absolute level of recreational spending (as opposed to its share in total spending) might continue to rise, despite the negative effects of hours reduction. Moreover, the distribution of the recreational dollar is likely to change, so that expenditures on certain recreational items will increase whether or not the total recreational budget rises. One of the more striking changes in recreational spending in the past forty years has been the increased share going to outdoor recreation at the expense of indoor recreation. But this reallocation is not so surprising when we consider changes in working hours, and hence in leisure time.

Much of the reallocation can be related to the trend toward larger leisure modules, noted earlier. This has provided a dramatic increase in the daytime leisure of American workers, and daytime leisure is spent in quite different ways than evening leisure. Time-budget data show that evening leisure is largely spent indoors, daytime leisure, outdoors. Hence, if the trend continues and a reduction in working hours is taken as a reduction in work days, a continued increase in recreational expenditures for outdoor recreation is likely.

This trend may also have implications for the level of recreational spending. Time budgets show that more than half of evening leisure time is spent watching television (a very inexpensive pastime), while much of the ambitious activity associated with the leisure revolution described in the popular press—boating, skiing, and so on—occurs in the daytime modules provided by weekends, holidays, and annual vacations. In the past, the tendency to spend relatively more time in outdoor activities as work time was reduced coincided with a strong upward trend in real income, which could support the more expensive diversions often associated with daytime leisure. A continuation of these several trends would also be well accommodated in the future with a scenario of high growth accompanied by hours reduction (the first scenario): at higher levels of income, an increased portion of income is available for discretionary purchases, and this could be spent on recreational goods and services.

But the low-growth scenario for hours reduction would require some variation from past recreational trends. With much more time off but with little or no gain in income, less money would be available to spend per hour of free time. If the trend toward larger leisure modules continued under these circumstances, one would predict a redirection of time toward a variety of inexpensive leisure activities. (For example, greater use of public parks near population centers, more picnicking and fishing.) One would expect a slowdown or reversal of the current trend toward upgrading evening leisure by the purchase of expensive new equipment (video cassettes and discs, giant screen television, high-fidelity sound systems, and so on). However, since the trend toward more daytime leisure may be reversed if work time reduction is imposed as a social policy, one might see no increase at all in spending on outdoor recreation activities in the second scenario.

Metropolitan Growth

A sharp reduction in working hours would affect where people live and work in metropolitan areas, as well as the location and nature of the types of services (recreational, shopping, and profession) they would demand. It would also affect urban transit variables, such as the average length of time spent commuting and the balance between mass and automotive transportation. And it would affect the relative growth of metropolitan areas, especially in the sunbelt and snowbelt.

The analysis of these effects is complicated, partly because factors that influence hours reduciton also influence various dimensions of metropolitan growth (see the appendix to this chapter). However, some rather straightforward predictions of the likely effect of hours reduction on metropolitan areas can be derived.

1. If work time reduction is spurred by increases in real hourly wages accompanied by a demand for more leisure (the first scenario), a shorter workweek would likely be associated with a more rapid expansion of metropolitan areas, as individuals took advantage of continued increases in purchasing power, less work time, and fewer commuting trips to locate further from their place of work; as employers moved to adjust to the new distribution of their (potential) labor force; and as retail trade and service establishments moved closer to their new markets. This would be most likely if a large portion of work time reduction took the form of fewer days worked per year (and hence fewer days of commuting). But even in this scenario, relatively less would be spent on housing and improvement in residential amenities.

2. In the second scenario, people have more time but smaller incomes. Hence, the effects on metropolitan expansion are still less certain. However, one might predict other impacts on metropolitan problems; for example, increased use of inexpensive commuting methods, such as buses, and longer commuting trips in those situations where increased distance from the center city enabled workers to buy residential land more cheaply, to purchase inexpensive homes, and to carry out a variety of do-it-yourself activities, ranging from home repair to vegetable gardening.

3. Turning to more specific effects of hours reduction, in the high-growth, leisure-oriented scenario, the expansion of those metropolitan areas that offer recreational amenities would be favored. Among other consequences, this would be expected to exacerbate the frost belt–sun belt competition. It would also offer advantages to newer metropolitan areas, which have the opportunity to develop urban neighborhoods and suburban communities around recreational amenities (a swimming pool, recreation center, and so forth) that older areas, which inherited a stock of residential capital built when the workweek was forty, fifty, or more hours, do not have. And medium-sized metropolitan areas could have an advantage over very large areas if the former had easier access to attractive outdoor recreation facilities.

4. The second-home movement would undoubtedly be spurred by hours reduction in the high-growth scenario. Certain areas (say, 50 to 200 miles from a large metropolitan area, providing recreational attractions such as mountains, lakes, or an ocean) might be utterly transformed if four-day, thirty- or thirty-two-hour workweeks became standard (consider, for example, the effect on southern Vermont and the Berkshires of a four-day workweek in New York City).

5. Urban transit systems would be affected, probably negatively. A reduction of 20 percent or more in the number of work-related trips, accompanied by a sharp increase in the number of trips for recreational, shopping, and other purposes, can be expected to reinforce trends away from

travel to central locations and toward more diffuse travel patterns. This would in turn help to further shift the balance away from mass transit (especially fixed-rail systems) and toward automobile usage. This impact would be most negative if employees on a thirty- or thirty-two-hour week typically worked the same four days (as they generally now work the same five days). Without staggered shifts, mass transit systems would be faced with idle machinery almost half the days of the year. Revenues would decline unless a sizable hike in fares were imposed, further reducing ridership. If an outward movement of people and jobs imposed demands for capital outlays for the construction of new commuter facilities, the fiscal pressure on mass transit systems would be great.

6. Other, more indirect effects of work time reduction could also be forecast, if in a more speculative mode. For example, in the high-growth scenario, reduction in work time, an increase in income, and a new movement to disperse residences and jobs would likely make government promotion of racial and class integration more difficult, as long as individuals continue to prefer living in segregated neighborhoods.

7. Prediction of these specific effects (cities more oriented to recreational amenities, second-home construction, and problems in the areas of urban transit and school integration) are all more difficult to make in a low-growth scenario. The rate of new construction would probably be lower in this scenario, and the rate at which these trends would progress might also be slowed on that account, despite the new stimulus afforded by increased leisure and fewer commuting trips.

Summary

A reduction in work time will have a number of long-term economic and social effects, in addition to its direct, negative impact on national output. In both scenarios, it will increase the fiscal problems of the government by reducing tax revenues more than spending. New forms of leisure will also make new demands on the government budget. Effects on the management of the nation's materials and energy resources are ambiguous. Other effects will depend on the scenario in which the reduction takes place.

In the first scenario, people have both more leisure and more income. Under these circumstances, some interesting benefits of enhanced leisure could be obtained, including more ambitious recreational activities, extensive vacation travel, second homes, and primary residences far from city centers and places of employment. In the second scenario, individuals have more time off from work and less income than they would prefer. A much smaller increase in leisure is likely, partly because the decline in labor supply will be less than the reduction in hours (since an increase in the number of job seekers is predicted) and partly because workers will use some of their time off in do-it-yourself activities. Funds will be lacking for the more ambitious recreational activities. There may even be a reversal of the trend toward larger leisure modules if such reversal better accommodates moonlighting, shiftwork, and increased effort, and if employers reward these productive adjustments.

Appendix to Chapter Thirteen

EFFECTS OF HOURS REDUCTION ON
METROPOLITAN AREA GROWTH

The analysis of the effects of hours reduction on the various dimensions of metropolitan area growth is very complicated, partly because the factors that influence the latter also influence the former. This is illustrated in figure 13.1.

The analysis of hours reduction on the left-hand side of the figure incorporates some of the factors discussed in part 1 of the text. The right-hand side of the figure presents a schematic analysis of the determination of one important urban problem, the outward spread of people and jobs. The variables in box *B* generally support this outward movement. Similarly, rising material living standards (and the purchasing power that accompanies this increase) and a rapidly growing population would be expected to increase the effective demand for land-using residences and amenities and to support the outward movement of people and jobs. The availability of materials and energy and the willingness of employees to spend time commuting would also contribute to this movement.

A reduction in work time would in itself be expected to support the outward expansion of people and jobs, for two reasons: because of increased demand for land-using recreational and other amenities as a direct result of increased leisure, and because of the reduction in the number of necessary commuter trips as the workweek was cut from five to four days.

But juxtaposing the left- and right-hand sides of the figure brings out the complexity involved in forecasting the impacts of likely changes in work schedules on metropolitan growth and begins to make clear the pitfalls of endeavoring to substitute simple common sense analysis for a less informal structure. There are some straightforward relations; some variables influence hours but not metropolitan variables (those in box *A*), while some influence metropolitan but not hours variables (those in box *B*). Moreover, some variables that operate on both metropolitan and hours variables have a positive effect on each, so that indirect effects will simply reinforce direct effects.

But other relations are more complex. For example, while a direct result

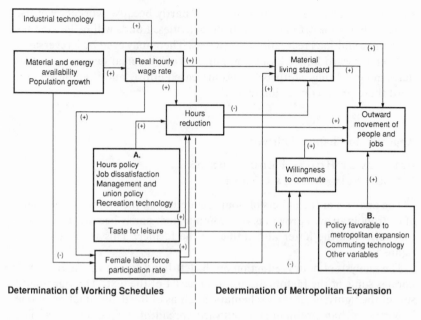

Determination of Working Schedules | Determination of Metropolitan Expansion

FIGURE 13.1. Effects of Hours Reduction on Metropolitan Area Growth

of hours reduction is predicted to be an outward movement of people and jobs, hours reduction would also reduce purchasing power, and hence the material living standard. This indirect effect would tend to undercut expansion.

Analysis of the effects of increases in real wage rates reveals an interesting result: a rapid increase in real wages would be likely to lead both to hours reduction and to a higher material living standard (in the past, hours reductions accompanying increases in hourly wages have never been enough to prevent some substantial increase in annual earnings). Hence, the effect of rapid growth in real wages would be unambiguously positive.

The figure also brings out interesting questions about the effects of other variables. An increasing taste for leisure would contribute to a decline in working hours but very possibly would strengthen resistance to spending time in commuting, so that the net effect on commuting time would be indeterminate. In the same way, an increase in female labor force participation would tend both to increase material living standards and to reduce weekly hours, thus supporting the outward movement in metropolitan areas; but two-earner families would have less time for household tasks and leisure (even if hours were cut somewhat) and so might be less willing to spend time commuting. Hence, it is not certain that an increase in female labor force participation would have a net positive effect on metropolitan area expansion.

PART IV

Implications of the Reduced Work Time Issue

CHAPTER FOURTEEN

Policy Considerations

THE WORK-LEISURE decision is fundamental to our lives. The allocation of time to the marketplace has wide-ranging implications for the economy, for a number of social issues, and for our personal concerns. It would be presumptuous to offer a recommendation about the appropriate hours of work time. In a democratic society, this outcome should reflect the interests and views of the more than one hundred million Americans who work in the marketplace and their employers.

But while recommendations concerning work time itself are not being made here, two areas of policy related to work time are discussed. The first concerns the possibility of an "unwanted" change in work schedules. An observer of long-term movements in the workweek cannot help but be concerned that an important change may take place in the average workweek as an indirect effect of other social phenomena, with the result that we find ourselves with a new set of working hours, and of laws regulating those hours, that the average employee and employer really do not want. For example, work time reductions taken because of persistently high unemployment are likely to become a permanent feature of the workplace despite individual preferences for more income rather than more leisure. Hence, it is appropriate to discuss policies that would minimize the likelihood of *unwanted* work time reductions.

A second area of concern arises from the need for policies that provide for optimal adjustment to reduced work time, if in fact working hours are cut. The discussion in part 2 of the possible economic costs of a shorter workweek made the point that the extent of the economic loss incurred could vary widely, depending upon a number of factors, including government policy. An effort is made here to bring out the implications of this analysis for the design of government policies to minimize economic loss if hours reduction does take place.

Preventing Unwanted Work Time Reduction

MAINTAINING FULL EMPLOYMENT

Full employment has many social and economic benefits, as well as some costs. A rarely mentioned benefit of a full-employment policy is that it would head off pressure for work sharing. A prolonged economic recession eventually generates an ideology that work opportunities are limited, which in turn can produce a gradually increasing chorus of demands that work opportunities be shared equitably, through a reduction in hours. The experience of the thirties and subsequent decades is that such work restrictions are apt to become permanent, even after full employment has been restored.

Demands for work sharing were muted in this country for some decades after World War II but then became insistent as unemployment levels crept upward in the 1970s. The same pattern has been observed in several European countries, where high unemployment has led to some work sharing and to demands for further reductions in hours. It is not implausible that a return to higher unemployment levels in the United States—at or above those of the early eighties—would lead to national legislation requiring a reduction in hours.

Admittedly, concern about work time restriction imposes just one more constraint on the economic policymaker, who already must maintain a difficult balance in dealing with the twin problems of unemployment and inflation. Still, it is not an unimportant consideration.

Other Forms of Labor Supply Restriction

In the depressed 1930s, women were admonished to remain at home, to provide more employment possibilities for male breadwinners. Today, that would be a politically unacceptable course, but we can encourage older employees to retire and we can discourage immigration from abroad. Both would reduce labor supply and hence could appear to be acceptable substitutes for work time reduction. However, this position is based on a defeatist attitude toward creating new employment opportunities and hence is also not acceptable. There may be other reasons for encouraging early retirement or for curbing immigration, but a lack of demand for labor is not a plausible basis. (Compare the long-term analysis of the demand for labor in part 3.)

Improving Work Incentives

A complementary factor encouraging work time reduction is the so-called decline of the work ethic, which may be related to government tax and expenditure policies. More specifically, it can be argued that government measures to bolster the income of the poor and to tax heavily the income of those with high earnings will reduce the financial incentive to work long hours. The relative importance of the present structure of tax and expenditure policies in reducing work incentives is, of course, controversial, but it is hard to argue with the view that, if a trend toward a welfare state were carried far enough, reduced work time and other measures of labor supply would suffer.

There are two ways in which this can occur. Welfare state institutions may reduce the incentives of individuals to supply effort to the market. They may then have a similar effect on groups of workers, such as trade unions. But these institutions may also condition the attitudes of workers toward national hours reduction legislation: if there is a widespread belief (based on experience at the firm or industry level) that only a marginal reduction in take-home pay occurs when hours, and hence gross weekly pay, are reduced, opposition to work time reduction legislation would be diminished. Of course, the reality is that if work time reduction is general, it will probably require an increase in the tax rate on earnings, and hence a sizable reduction in take-home pay, to obtain the needed funding for the continuation of welfare state programs. But, as we have seen, Europeans report that such clear understanding of the tax rate effects of work time reduction is unusual, even in countries where the welfare state is extensive and of long standing.

Because of these various difficulties, it is not easy to suggest a corrective policy. Still, an effort can be made. For example, incentive effects can be given a higher priority when designing new welfare state programs. For example, those subsidies to the poor which encourage them to make pro-ductivity-augmenting investments in themselves (e.g., education and training, or seed money for new enterprises) can be favored. Such subsidies yield the recipients a higher income only in proportion to the number of hours worked for pay, and so are believed to encourage effort.[1]

IMPROVING JOB DESIGN AND WORKING CONDITIONS

Both the nature of work and employee job satisfaction are likely to be important determinants of future reductions in work time. At the present time, specialists in personnel management have a variety of tools to make work more pleasant and satisfying. These include, on the one hand, out-lays to improve the physical amenities of the workplace and, on the other hand, changes in the work itself, designed to improve its intrinsic interest: for example, job rotation, job enlargement, and matrix management.

Of course, some attempts to make work more pleasant will also make it less efficient. In fact, an effort to reduce job dissatisfaction and hence avoid a decline in hours of work could, in principle, be as costly as a reduc-tion in hours. The evaluation of the feasibility and efficacy of specific changes in job design and working conditions lies well beyond issues usu-ally addressed by the labor economist. However, changes in the scheduling of work and their likely impact on average hours worked is a topic somewhat closer to the traditional interests of the economist. Some possible changes in this area are discussed in the next section.

REFORMING WORK SCHEDULES

Work schedules can be made more flexible so that those who find the standard workweek unacceptable can have a different schedule, making it unnecessary to reduce the hours of the majority who are satisfied with the current schedule. The simplest accommodation is flexitime, which gives employees some freedom in selecting their beginning and ending hours of work. Flexitime has become increasingly common in the United States.

A more ambitious program allows the employee some choice over the number as well as over the timing of his hours. This system requires considerably more administrative effort on the part of management (partly because of its implications for the hourly cost of fringe benefits). It is apparently found in only a few employment sites.[2] Nevertheless, it is a possible alternative to a general change in the workweek.

Reducing the Economic Costs of Work Time Reduction

Appropriate government and private sector policies could mitigate the negative economic effects of a reduction in hours of work. Clearly, the efficacy of policies to minimize output loss must depend upon the scenario in which they are introduced: if hours are reduced for social reasons, despite widespread interest by individuals in maintaining their material living standards (the second scenario), one would expect greater success than if the reduction occurs simply because the average worker wants more leisure and is willing to make a substantial economic sacrifice to achieve it (the first scenario).

But aggressive policy could have a positive payoff in either case. Even when the average worker opts for more leisure, one can expect that a minority will be more susceptible to economic incentives. Today, tens of millions of Americans moonlight, work overtime, or put in long hours at their own business, despite the satisfaction of the majority with a forty-hour workweek. A similar diversity of tastes could be expected if the nation moved to a thirty- or thirty-two-hour workweek under affluent conditions.

Policies to minimize output loss due to hours reduction could further three major goals: increase the number of people working, intensify hourly effort, and maintain capital utilization through an increase in shiftwork.

Increasing Labor Force Participation

A shorter workweek obviously could permit higher labor force participation, but managerial policies must be designed to foster, not hinder, this result. For example, the shorter workweek could be scheduled at times convenient to mothers of young children. It can be argued that the optimal schedule would be a workweek coincident with that used by the public schools. But this in turn raises the question of whether our present public school schedules make sense: many critics have pointed out that these schedules were designed to meet the requirements of nineteenth-century America—especially the need of agriculture for child labor in the summer and in the late afternoon and early morning—but now appear to be an anachronism in our urban, postindustrial society. If workweeks and work years for adults are significantly reduced, the argument for synchronization of adult and school schedules will become much stronger. A four-day, seven-and-a-half-hour day workweek in the schools, combined with a significant increase in the number of days attended per year, would permit the coordination of child and adult schedules if the adult workweek were reduced to thirty hours.

Similarly, a reduced workweek would be complementary with efforts to extend work life by deferring retirement and by permitting young people to attend college while working full time. These goals would be facilitated by such policies as changing (or eliminating) the earnings test for Social Security benefits and by revising student aid formulas to provide more assistance to students working full time.

Increasing Effort on the Job

An increase in labor productivity might be obtainable with a cut in hours for two reasons. First, fatigue may be less, and fewer work breaks may be needed. Second, union-management productivity bargaining could be expected to be more fruitful. Such bargaining would probably be more successful in the second scenario, where workers are reluctant to sacrifice their material living standards for an increase in leisure.

Maintaining or Improving Capital Utilization

If hours were reduced, capital utilization could be improved through greater use of both conventional and unconventional shift work. Examples of the latter include the use of a part-time shift after the full-time shift leaves. As another example, a three-day weekend shift of seven-and-a-half to ten hours per day could complement a four-day, seven-and-a-half-hour-day standard workweek, improving capital utilization without imposing any additional evening or night work. Or, one can have two five-day, six-hour-a-day shifts (for example, 6 A.M. to 12 P.M. and 12 P.M. to 6 P.M.) or, alternatively, three-day, ten-hour-a-day shifts. These schedules could also be supplemented by overtime and by night work, to further improve capital utilization. Of course, it is much easier to design shift schedules that would satisfy the engineering requirements of the plant than it is to predict whether workers will be interested in applying for them.[3] Here, too, the scenario approach is useful, in that one would predict less willingness to work inconvenient shifts in the first scenario, where hours reduction is a result of a general desire to subordinate material living standards to leisure time and related concerns.

But government policy can also play a role. It was noted in chapter 12 that close observers of shiftwork patterns have concluded that an important determinant of employees' acceptance of shifts is the level of amenities available during nonworking hours. Hence, government can stimulate shift work (and at the same time make the lives of shift workers less difficult, thus reducing the social cost of shift work) by fostering a social infrastructure that better serves the evening or night worker. Government policies to serve this goal might:

- provide all-night programming on television and other government-regulated media;
- eliminate local ordinances that limit the hours of operation of retail trade and service establishments (including bars and taverns);
- subsidize the twenty-four-hour-a-day, seven-day-a-week operation of semipublic or public athletic centers;
- support all-night movie houses;
- provide special police protection for nighttime users of these facilities;
- control daytime noise in residential areas. For example, in some European industrial towns where shift work is extensive, a portion of publicly supported housing must be effectively soundproofed. This housing is offered to shift workers at subsidized rates.

Chapter One. The United States

1. Foss, *Changing Utilization of Fixed Capital,* table 1, pp. 8–10.
2. Ibid.
3. The details were obtained from the U.S. Department of Labor, *Current Population Survey.* A similarity of hours of full-time employees between the service and goods-producing sectors emerges from the breakdown by both industry and occupation. (These data are not directly comparable to the establishment data cited above, since they include the hours of moonlighters.) Occupational data are found in U.S. Department of Labor, *Employment and Earnings,* June 1986, table A-11.
4. U.S. Department of Labor, *Employment and Earnings,* June 1986, table A-3.
5. Stinson, "Moonlighting by Women."
6. See McDonald, "Underground Economy." For example, McDonald stated: "One group of underground workers includes those people with regular employment, but who also enter the underground sector through moonlighting or whatever. These workers have a clear incentive to report their regular sector activities to the CPS interviewer, as this is the course that (in the respondent's eyes) would arouse the least suspicion" (p. 12).
7. U.S. Department of Labor, *Employment and Earnings,* June 1985, table A-30; U.S. Department of Labor, *Current Population Survey,* October 1985.
8. The data used in the figures in this chapter and the following chapters are discussed in the appendixes to these chapters.
9. See Owen, *Working Hours,* and Owen, *Working Lives,* for attempts to deal with this question. On the one hand, we know that the female labor force includes an increasing proportion of mothers with small children and that this group spends more time in housework than do other women. On the other hand, we know that there have been improvements in timesavers in the home and, from fragmentary evidence, that there have been changes in attitudes toward doing housework that would predict less time spent at it. There is also reason to expect a cyclical movement in housework time, highly correlated with the number of children: the average number of children per woman rose during the baby boom period and for some years since, but then declined sharply. Some direct evidence of a decline in housework and an increase in leisure as the number of children to be cared for fell is found in a comparison of data for 1965 and 1975. See Juster and Stafford, *Time, Goods, and Well-Being.*
10. See below for an adjustment for annual vacations and holidays. Since this measure excludes proprietors and farmers, and since these work longer hours

than nonagricultural wage and salary employees, it overestimates the amount of leisure enjoyed by the average nonstudent male who is employed. Since the fraction of the labor force that is self-employed or in agriculture has declined, changes in this measure underestimate the increase in leisure that has occurred.

11. An imperfection in both series is that they do not measure coffee breaks and other work breaks. Compare the discussion in the appendix.

12. The appendix contains a discussion of the sources of vacation and holiday data and their use in constructing the estimates in the text.

13. See appendix.

14. The vacation and holiday data are for all demographic groups, not just nonstudent males. Vacation and holiday data for students are lacking. However, it is likely that students receive less vacation time than do adults. Assuming that students obtain no vacation time at all, one obtains a downward bias in the hours-per-week adjustment of 0.15 hours. Hence the bias is between 0 and 0.15 hours per week. Data are available on the sex breakdown of vacations, and these indicate that women enjoy significantly more vacation time than men. Indeed, since the bias of including women exceeds that due to including students in this measure, one obtains a net upward bias.

15. See Kunze, "New BLS Survey," p. 3.

16. Stafford and Duncan, "Use of Time and Technology," p. 254. Their estimate includes lunch time in excess of one hour as well as break time of 43 minutes.

17. Ibid., p. 250.

18. Stafford and Cohen, "Model of Work Effort and Productive Consumption."

19. Ure, *Philosophy of Manufactures.*

20. U.S. Department of Labor, *Employee Benefits in Medium and Large Firms,* table 5.

21. For male and female nonagricultural employees, average job tenure is, respectively, 3.7 and 2.6 years. See Sekscenski, *Job Tenure Declines as Work Force Changes,* table 5.

22. U.S. Department of Labor, *Employee Benefits in Medium and Large Firms,* p. 4.

23. This requires that data on part-week and full-week vacations be combined.

24. See Henle, "Recent Growth of Paid Leisure." Henle compared a month in which the survey was taken to include a holiday with the same month in adjacent years and concluded that a 20 percent adjustment was needed.

25. This figure is obtained by adding to the full-week vacation estimate a full-week equivalent estimate for part-week vacations. The latter is obtained by taking the ratio of average hours worked by those on part-week vacations for those usually working full time to average full-time hours.

26. Henle, "Recent Growth of Paid Leisure," p. 4.

27. Telephone interview with Kent Kunze, economist, Office of Productivity and Technology, BLS, May 13, 1987. The most recent published data are for 1983. See Kunze, "Hours at Work Increase Relative to Hours Paid."

28. See Kunze, "New BLS Survey."

29. See Klein, "Missed Work and Lost Hours." The survey of nonagricultural workers showed 1.6 percent of working hours missed for illness and 1.1 per-

cent missed for miscellaneous reasons. The *CPS* data indicate that 43.7 percent of sick time and 27.87 percent of miscellaneous time not at work was paid. Multiplying the two sets of figures and adding them together gives 1 percent.

30. However, ignoring these incidents does mean that subtracting the employee absence figure of 1 percent from the paid-time-off estimate of 6.5 percent to obtain 5.5 percent of total work time for paid vacations and holidays is a slight overestimate.

31. Henle, "Recent Growth of Paid Leisure," p. 254.

32. Numbers in thousands of employees.

33. Note that these data differ from those presented in Owen, *Working Hours.* The significant difference between the two series is that the earlier work adjusted weekly hours for the growth in vacations and holidays. (In the historical series presented there, the adjustment was zero for 1940 and earlier years.) The adjusted series presented here takes into account the downward effect on the level of hours of the basic holidays offered even in the war or prewar periods.

Chapter Two. Western Europe

1. Unpublished data from U.S. Department of Labor, Bureau of Labor Statistics, June 1987; interview with Arthur Neef, director, International Comparisons Division, BLS, July 15, 1987.

2. The data in table 2.2 are based on calculations by the West German research organization Institut fur Arbeit und Berufsforschung. (The following description of the IAB's methodology is based on Reyher, "Draft Report on Hours Worked.") The IAB begins with data on annual hours for manual workers (for which more complete data are available), then builds up to estimates for non-manual workers, using available data. The estimates first obtain the number of normal hours of work per week as agreed by trade unions and employer associations, or with individual firms, or as fixed by legal regulations. These data are then adjusted for overtime, vacations and holidays, sick leave, and other work time losses, including those due to short-time working, bad weather, strikes and lockouts, and absenteeism. They are also adjusted for part-time work. In 1983, the IAB reported that 30 percent of the female work force in West Germany and 12 percent of its total work force worked part time and averaged twenty-three hours a week.

3. *IDS/PA European Report* 289; May 5, 1987.

4. The difference may be due in part to the German practice of extending union benefits to nonunion workers. But see, below, the more general discussion of U.S.-European differences.

5. In addition, supplementary holiday pay is now received by 94 percent of German employees. For approximately two-thirds of all employees, this amounts to one full month's pay. "On average, supplementary holiday and annual bonus combined amounted to 92% of a month's pay for each employee per year." *IDS/PA European Report* 289, May 5, 1987, p. iii.

6. These are hours offered by employers: standard or normal hours plus overtime and net of short time. Part-timers (in this context, those working part time voluntarily) are excluded from the establishment survey, giving it an upward bias. A recent study estimated the proportion of voluntary part-timers in the labor force at 5.5 percent. See Combault, "Le travail à temps partiel en 1984." These workers fit the following definition of part-time employment: "on hiring, [it] is agreed with the employer to work at a schedule less than that normal in the establishment. . . . Those in an establishment that are on partial unemployment should not be considered as part-time" (p. 146). However, French analyses of the series say that it has a downward bias because of the way the data are collected. Employers give data for groups of their employees, rather than for individuals, and may exclude individuals or subgroups who work longer than usual hours.

7. INSEE, "La Durée annuelle du travail 1970–1983." Another study, Frayssinet, "La Durée annuelle du travail en 1981 et 1982," reported on a survey of employers of ten or more employees in private industry and commerce. This study excluded temporary employees and part-timers. Data were not adjusted for time lost due to sickness, bad weather, or strikes. The Frayssinet study found that working hours per year in 1982 averaged 1,810. In 1981, they were calculated at 1,873.

8. Data obtained from U.S. Department of Labor, July 15, 1987.

9. Blyton, *Changes in Working Time*, pp. 21–22.

10. "Recent Changes in Hours," p. 131.

11. Robinson, "Changing Labor Market," p. 19.

12. Blyton, *Changes in Working Time*, p. 78. Also, see Blyton, pp. 77–81, for statements on vacations in Great Britain. See *Employment Gazette* for further statistics on British vacations.

13. Unpublished British government data received from Patricia Cap de Ville, U.S. Department of Labor, July 15, 1987.

Chapter Three. The United States and Western Europe: A Comparison

1. International comparisons of data on weekly working hours are also made difficult because the statistical average of hours in each country has been reduced by an influx of female part-timers. This movement may indicate a decrease as readily as an increase in the amount of leisure time enjoyed by the work force and hence is hard to interpret.

2. See Weber, "Federal Republic of Germany."

3. This provides an incentive for high-seniority workers as well as for beginners to remain with the company. If a high-seniority American worker leaves his employment, he knows he must make do with much less vacation time in his new job, even if he is moving to a better paid position.

Chapter Four. Arguments for Government Intervention

1. These three categories—market failure, redistribution, and macroeconomic benefit—are often used by economists to advocate government intervention in the economy.
2. A classic statement of this view is given in Pigou, *Economics of Welfare,* chap. 7. See especially Pigou's explanation of uneconomically long hours:

   > The apparent paradox is, however, easily explained. First, workpeople, in considering for what hours per day they will consent to work, often fail to take account of the damage that unduly long hours may do to their efficiency. Their lack of forethought in this matter is on a par with the general inability of all classes adequately to foresee future happenings in themselves, as distinguished to future happenings to themselves. Secondly, employers also often fail to realize that shorter hours would promote efficiency among their workpeople, and so would redound to their own interest. Thirdly—and this, on their side, is the principal thing—except in firms which possess a practical monopoly in some department of industry, and so expect to retain the same hands permanently, the lack of durable connection between individual employers and their workpeople makes it to the employers' interest to work longer hours than are in the long run to the interest of production as a whole. (p. 466)

   For another useful discussion of these issues, see the contemporary treatment by Cahill, *Shorter Hours.* Cahill adds yet another point in his review of the health argument for shorter hours: "The . . . argument that leisure provided health has been made to bear on citizenship by stressing the need of a strong race for defensive purposes" (p. 14).
3. This is said to be especially likely in the case of poorly paid workers who also lack a financial reserve. But see Owen, *Working Hours,* for a discussion of an opposite possibility: that workers making semisubsistence wages may work too *little* and so underinvest in the nutrition and housing of themselves and their families.
4. Again, a classic statement is found in Pigou: "Where mobility and trade union organization are imperfect and where, therefore . . . there is some range of indeterminateness in the bargain between an employer and his workpeople, the employer's bargaining power, as against his workpeople, is greater in the matter of hours of labour than it is in the matter of wages. For, whereas a workman striving to get better wages has only, as it were, to lift his own weight, it is, as a rule, impossible, for technical reasons, that any concession about the hours of labour should be made to him that is not general in character, and, therefore, less willingly granted" (*Economics of Welfare,* p. 467).
5. Thus, Pigou concludes: "What has been said is sufficient to constitute a prima facie case for State intervention" (ibid., p. 468).
6. In Germany, the limit is sixty per week, although exceptions are allowed for emergencies. In addition, legal and union restrictions are often imposed in Europe on the total number of hours that can be worked by an individual in a month, quarter, or year.

7. See the discussion of the importance of productive consumption in the labor-leisure choice under semisubsistence conditions in Owen, *Working Hours.*

8. Another reason is given by White, *Working Hours: Assessing the Potential,* who pointed out that employers often time a reduction in hours with the introduction of a labor-saving technology in order to reduce layoffs (chap. 5). Where true, this could induce an overly optimistic view among workers of the effects of hours reduction.

9. See Gunton, *Wealth and Progress;* Gunton, *Principles of Social Progress;* and Cahill, *Shorter Hours.* Cahill discusses the role of Gunton and Steward in the shorter-hours movement.

10. Cahill, *Shorter Hours,* p. 16.

11. Ibid., p. 16.

12. However, increased female labor force participation has reduced the supply of volunteers for political and other organizations.

13. See Ford, "Why I Favor Five Days Work."

14. See Owen, *Price of Leisure.*

15. However, the resulting fall in income might, if regarded as temporary by the worker, yield an increase in the proportion of income consumed, according to the permanent income theory of consumption.

16. Northrup and Brinberg, *Economics of the Workweek.*

17. Weber, "Federal Republic of Germany," p. 9.

18. Ibid., p. 12.

19. Nemirow, "Work-Sharing Approaches."

20. See Gutchess, *Employment Security in Action.* The policy also calls for appropriate inventory variation, product diversity, and labor hoarding (discussed in chapter 6).

21. A partial exception is provided in states where there is a system of full-experience rating (so that a firm's insurance premium is raised in proportion to the amount of unemployment it has caused).

22. Another, perhaps more compelling, reason, though, is the greater cost in Europe of using the alternative of employment fluctuations because of the high cost of dismissing an employee.

Chapter Five. Offsets to Government Intervention

1. Ashenfelter, "Compliance with the Minimum Wage Law."

2. Ehrenberg and Schumann, *Longer Hours or More Jobs?,* p. 136.

3. Best, *Work Sharing,* p. 129.

4. I am assuming that this does not have deleterious effects on the quality and performance of the work force or on the ability of the employer to recruit workers.

5. For example, see Ehrenberg, *Fringe Benefits and Overtime Behavior.*

6. See Hart, *Working Time and Employment,* for an excellent summary of this argument.

7. There may also be a scale effect, which operates to reduce both hours and employment. The lower standard workweek, with the consequent higher daily

wage bill, raises labor costs overall, and this will tend, ceteris paribus, to result in a lower amount of labor employed. Compare the discussion in chapter 8.

8. For an excellent treatment of the possible effect of a higher overtime premium see Ehrenberg and Schumann, *Longer Hours or More Jobs?* See also the very useful discussion in Best, *Work Sharing.*

9. Santamaki-Vuori, "Cyclical Adjustment of Hours and Employment."

10. There have also been miscellaneous objections to the argument that a reduction in the standard workweek would reduce hours. Several economists have pointed out that a significant portion of the work force now puts in less than thirty-five hours a week and so would not be affected. The self-employed and exempt employees would also not be affected. It has also been argued that a reduction in the standard workweek would induce many women to move from part-time to full-time status—that is, to increase their hours of work. See Dagsvik et al., "Impact on Labor Supply of a Shorter Workday."

11. Lewis, "Hours of Work and Hours of Leisure." In this context, Lewis did not consider other special influences operative in this period, including the introduction of five-day weeks by many employers in the 1930s as a response to the Depression, or the rapid spread of industrial unionism in the late thirties and early forties, accompanied by demands for a forty-hour week. Lewis also compared the 1929–42 period with the 1942–55 period and made three observations. First, in industries covered by the FLSA, hours reduction was much slower in the second period than in the first. Second, in the later period, hours reduction was slower in covered than in uncovered industries. And third, many manufacturing employees worked forty hours a week (the standard workweek under FLSA). These observations would be consistent with the regulation having a continuing, if more moderate, influence on hours.

12. Hart, *Working Time and Employment.*

13. Hart and Wilson, "Demand for Workers and Hours."

14. Ehrenberg and Schumann, *Longer Hours or More Jobs?*

15. Ibid.

16. A less extreme tactic is to impose maximum levels of overtime that can be worked by an employee in a given period (a week, month, quarter, or year, for example). Such constraints are sometimes included in labor contracts, especially in Western Europe.

17. During World War II, for example, a commitment to a social goal (the defeat of the Axis powers) was sufficient to induce Americans to accept departures from free-market outcomes in many areas of everyday life. Evasions and exemptions did exist then, of course, but they did not prevent the successful pursuit of the national goal.

Chapter Six. The Firm's Economic Efficiency

1. For examples of empirical estimates of labor hoarding, see Fair, "Excess Labor and the Business Cycle"; and Chang, "Econometric Model of the Short Run Demand."

2. Fay and Medoff, "Labor and Output over the Business Cycle."

3. Compare the discussion in ibid.

4. In that event, all the benefit of the work-sharing program is in the form of higher profits for the firm (at the cost of slimmer pay packets for its workers).

5. According to this interpretation, the nineteenth-century employer would have obtained more output from his work force if he had reduced hours of work. This alleged error could have resulted from the ignorance of earlier entrepreneurs of modern personnel methods for obtaining more from one's staff or (somewhat more plausibly) from neglect by employers of the long-term effects of long hours on health, and hence productivity. The latter argument becomes more persuasive when one considers the high rates of turnover common among employees in newly industrialized sectors. However, it neglects the other side of the income-leisure choice: if shorter hours in that period had, in the short run, meant smaller weekly earnings, the nutrition and housing of the work force would have been reduced. A reduction in nutrition and housing for workers at the semisubsistence level means lower productivity in the future. Hence, a reduction in hours will have both negative and positive effects on future productivity. It is not obvious which will be dominant.

   A third explanation was offered by Christoph Deutschmann, who emphasized that employment for German workers in that period was most irregular—partly because of recurrent power failures, machinery breakdowns, and material shortfalls—so that they had frequent opportunities to obtain the leisure to recoup their energy, despite long *scheduled* hours. Author interview with Deutschmann, Berlin, September 1986, based on Deutschmann's ongoing research.

6. See, for example, Brown, "Hours and Output"; and Commission of the European Communities, "Adaptation of Working Time." See White, *Working Hours: Assessing the Potential,* for another view.

7. See Brown, "Hours and Output," and the references cited there.

8. See the papers in Singleton, Fox, and Whitfield, *Measurement of Man at Work,* especially Bonjer, "Temporal Factors and Physiological Load," and Murrell, "Temporal Factors in Light Work." See also Snook and Irvine, "Psychophysical Studies of Physiological Fatigue Criteria," and the sources cited in note 6 above.

9. See, for example, Lazear, "Agency, Earnings Profiles, Productivity and Hours Restrictions"; and Shapiro and Stiglitz, "Equilibrium Unemployment."

10. Exceptions to this result should be noted. For example, the fact that reduced work time reduces future income obtained by keeping one's job reduces the employee's incentive to work harder in order to lower the probability of losing his job. This may induce some workers to reduce, not increase, their work effort.

11. Compare the work of Abraham Maslow, of Frederick Herzberg and his followers, and of Lea, Tarpy, and Webley, *Individual in the Economy,* especially chapter 6. See also Filer, "People and Productivity"; and MacFadyen, "Motivational Constructs in Psychology."

12. Karl Marx himself put considerable emphasis on the employers' effort to "increase the intensity of labor" to offset the tendency for the rate of profit to fall as capital became less scarce in an industrializing society. A number of mod-

ern Marxians have continued to stress the importance of the workplace struggle over employee effort. Indeed, one of the most telling criticisms by radicals of standard neoclassical economics was its neglect until recently of the effort issue. (Most of the neoclassical research mentioned above dates back less than ten years.) However, radical scholars have been quick to adapt the new neoclassical work to their own ends.

13. Bowles, "Production Process in the Competitive Economy."

14. Thus, see Edwards, *Contested Terrain,* and Burawoy, *Manufacturing Consent.*

15. It is important to separate the effect of an hours reduction from that of high unemployment. One of the theories cited above related effort to the power exerted by the employer in the workplace. This theory would then predict an increase in employee effort when unemployment is high. But one may then question the impact of employer power on the work time–work effort relation and ask whether employers couldn't use their improved bargaining power to demand more from their employees without any cut in hours.

   However, the question is not so simple. A number of writers have told us that a company may maximize its long-time profits by *not* taking maximum advantage of its bargaining power vis-à-vis its work force during a slump: there are long-term gains to be had from projecting an image of fairness to the workers. But a reduction in hours can provide the employer with a plausible excuse to demand a change in the customary amount of work required per hour, without appearing to be taking unfair advantage of the bad labor market. (The firm could claim simply that the shorter day left the worker less fatigued and so with a greater amount of energy to be applied when he was at work.)

   In the second place, if the work-sharing policy is imposed on the work group from without, by national laws or by industrywide union bargaining, then the employer and the employees acting together may seek to use increased effort per hour as a way of sabotaging an unwanted policy—by maintaining the workers' income and the employer's output. (To obtain this result, the employer will of course have to offer some increased monetary compensation for extra effort.) For these reasons, an industrial relations theory that stressed power and informal bargaining arrangements might well predict that a cut in hours would yield an increase in hourly effort in excess of that resulting from the recession.

16. In the more theoretical literature, this distinction has led some writers to argue that, while increases in employment, holding capital stock constant, yield diminishing returns (the textbook case), increases in hours per worker do not. If this one-man-one-machine view of the effects of hours reduction is accepted, the substitution of hours reduction for employment reduction will yield an increase in the number of working hours per unit of output. In other words, a given percentage reduction in hours will require a larger percentage increase in staff, if output is to be maintained.

17. Stafford and Cohen, "Model of Work Effort and Productive Consumption."

18. See Marchand, Rault, and Turpin, "Des 40 heures aux 39 heures." See also Franz, "Is Less More?", for a discussion of employer plans. British experience

with work time reduction is described at length in White, *Working Hours: Assessing the Potential.* White also included useful descriptions of Continental experience.

19. See White, *Working Hours: Assessing the Potential,* for a description of British experience.

20. Leveson, "Reduction in Hours of Work."

21. See also Poper, "Critical Evaluation," for a useful review of 1,677 cases of hours reduction. Poper points out further methodological difficulties in measuring the effects of hours reduction on output. He concluded that, while hours reduction may have improved productivity when hours were long, "a distinct possibility exists that weekly hours materially below forty will have effects opposite to those originally intended" (p. 139). In Poper's view, as a result of strenuous activities outside the workplace, "workers may reach levels of fatigue approximating those which existed prior to the curtailment of hours [below forty]."

22. See Feldstein, "Specification of the Labour Input"; Craine, "On the Service Flow from Labor"; and Leslie and Wise, "Productivity of Hours."

23. This is true despite the reduced fatigue caused by shorter schedules and the fear factor—the positive productivity effect of higher unemployment.

24. White, *Working Hours: Assessing the Potential.*

25. But see the more negative evaluation in chapter 11, based on evidence from the market for part-time workers.

Chapter Seven. Effects on Wages

1. In the long-run analysis presented in part 3, prices are assumed to be fully adjusted to wages. Hence, real wages rather than money wages are of interest there.

2. Jallade, "Reduction and Adjustment of Working Time."

3. Useful models are contained in Calmfors, "Employment Policies, Wage Formation, and Trade Union Behavior"; Calmfors, "Work Sharing, Employment, and Wages"; Calmfors and Hoel, "Work Sharing, Overtime, and Shiftwork"; Hoel, "Short- and Long-Run Effects of Reduced Working Time"; Hoel, "Can Shorter Working Time Reduce Unemployment?"; Hoel, "Employment and Allocation Effects"; Hoel and Vale, "Effects of Reduced Working Time"; Booth and Schiantarelli, "Employment Effects of a Shorter Working Week"; Oswald, "Economic Theory of Trade Unions"; Pencavel, "Wages and Employment under Trade Unionism"; Franz, "Is Less More?"; and Hart, *Working Time and Employment.* These microeconomic models also underlie the static analysis of firm behavior presented in the following chapter.

4. See Hoel and Vale, "Effects of Reduced Working Time."

5. Of course, the reduced weekly earnings offered in the market, as a result of hours reduction, will lower the financial return to an investment in job search. This would, other things being equal, reduce search activity.

6. For example, the United Kingdom briefly adopted a shorter workweek in the 1970s, to save energy. While hourly rated employees generally did not have

their hourly wage increased, those on monthly or annual salary—essentially, the white collar work force—did not have their salaries cut. Hence, they were given a generous increase in their hourly rate. (This differential treatment was said to lower morale among blue collar workers, and so to be a major factor in the abandonment of the scheme.)

7. See note 3.

8. The International Typographers Union has often been taken as an example of a strong U.S. union in an industry of small firms, and its wage-setting policies has been studied with the help of this model.

9. The models vary as to the number of individuals with whom the union is concerned. It might be just current employees; all voting members (many unions permit workers laid off in the recent past to vote); all those who have been employed, including all the laid off (or those laid off in some stated period of time, perhaps greater than that which would permit them to maintain voting privileges); those who might be employed (e.g., the young, minorities, and women) if employment were to increase; or all the unemployed in the economy. Or it may be assumed that the union's politics are largely dominated by older, high-seniority workers who have little fear of layoffs and are not concerned about the rest of the members. In general, the wider the definition of workers about whom the union is concerned, the more weight given in the model to the welfare of the unemployed.

10. This follows from an assumption of diminishing marginal utility of income. If income is reduced, its marginal utility is increased, increasing the weight given to income gain in union decision making.

11. Compare the discussion of long-term effects in Hoel, "Short- and Long-Run Effects."

12. It is important to note here that these models do not consider the effect of higher unemployment rates on the unemployment insurance costs that may fall on employed workers. Compare the discussion in part 3.

13. Booth and Schiantarelli, "Employment Effects of a Shorter Working Week."

14. Insofar as the reduction in hours leads to a decline in total working hours and hence in the tax base for unemployment insurance, the tax rate would be increased. However, if the program is moderately successful in avoiding layoffs, this secondary effect is likely to be dominated by the reduction in unemployment. Hence, an increase in the actual rate is not likely.

Chapter Eight. The Firm's Employment Decision

1. The static microeconomic analysis in this chapter draws heavily from the contributions in publications cited in note 3 of the previous chapter.

2. See Calmfors and Hoel, "Worksharing, Overtime, and Shiftwork."

3. See the discussion in note 16 of chapter 6.

4. Compare the discussion in chapter 6.

5. If diminishing returns from hours of work just equals the diminishing returns from number of employees, then a reduction in hours requires an equiproportionate increase in the number of employees to keep output constant.

6. This simple approach assumes that the firm regards both the wage paid to labor and the price obtained for output as constants. This would be a valid assumption if competition is assumed. Then even if changes in hours and employment yielded changes in wages and prices, the firm would regard them as exogenous variables. But if the firm's employment and output decisions do influence wages and prices, then the profit maximization condition becomes

$$MP_L = (w/p)\, x,$$

where $x = (1 + E_{w,L})/(1 + E_{P,O})$, and E denotes elasticity. Then the relative change in the marginal product of labor must equal the sum of the relative changes in the wage-price ratio and in x.

7. An exception arises if demand is sufficiently inelastic. This can be illustrated with the help of production function two, a simple if somewhat extreme case. In that function, a reduction in hours yields a proportionate decline in output and no change in the hourly productivity of an additional worker. Employment changes would depend only on the change in the ratio of wages to prices. If demand is inelastic, a decline in hours (yielding a proportionate decline in output) induces a more than proportionate increase in price. But wages need only change in proportion to hours to keep purchasing power constant. Hence, a cut in hours might yield a greater change in price than in wages and so reduce the wage-price ratio. Then employment increases in this model, while the purchasing power of the worker remains intact.

8. See for example, Franz, "Is Less More?"; and Marchand, Rault, and Turpin, "Des 40 heures aux 39 heures."

Chapter Nine. National Economic Effects

1. For useful macroeconomic analyses, see van Ginneken, "Employment and the Reduction of the Workweek"; Allen, "Economic Effects of a Shorter Working Week"; Henize, "Evaluation of the Effects of a Reduction in Working Hours"; Henize, "Can a Shorter Workweek Reduce Unemployment?"; Oudiz, Raoul, and Sterdyniak, "Reduire la durée du travail"; Marchand, Rault, and Turpin, "Des 40 heures aux 39 heures"; Whitley and Wilson, "Macroeconomic Merits of a Marginal Employment Subsidy"; Whitley and Wilson, "Impact on Employment of Reduction in the Length of the Working Week"; and Whitley and Wilson, "Hours Reductions within Large-Scale Macroeconomic Models."

2. Note that an accommodating monetary policy does not prevent a decline in the real income of employed workers. For example, if unions responded to a 10 percent decrease in the workweek by demanding, and getting, a 10 percent increase in their hourly wage, but the monetary authorities responded by accommodating a 10 percent increase in prices, the real hourly wages of workers would be unchanged, and the purchasing power of the originally employed workers would have been cut by 10 percent.

3. Since these models contain lagged effects, it is typical to assess the effect of

hours reduction over a period of time, often lasting several years. The period is divided into conventional periods (e.g., a quarter or three months), which are referred to as rounds.

4. Van Ginneken, "Employment and the Reduction of the Workweek."
5. Ibid., pp. 42–43. See also chapter 6.
6. See Marchand, Rault, and Turpin, "Des 40 heures aux 39 heures."
7. Compare the discussion in Hart, *Working Time and Employment.* Dreze, "Work Sharing," criticizes these simulations for being based on long-term time series rather than on specific recession conditions. This argument is of course quite consistent with those made in the last three chapters on the importance of the constellation of economic and social conditions in determining responses by employers, employees, unions, and governments to hours reduction.
8. Whitley and Wilson, "Impact on Employment."
9. Emerson, *Europe's Stagflation.*
10. Hoel, "Can Shorter Working Time Reduce Unemployment?" p. 13.
11. Chapter 8 analyzed the effects of hours reduction in the microeconomic context of the firm or industry. This chapter discusses macroeconomic effects at the economywide level. There is also an intermediate level of analysis: by broad sector. For example, one can divide the economy into two sectors, the formal and informal (or the legal and underground) and predict that a government policy of compulsory hours reduction will enlarge the second sector at the expense of the first. In a very interesting paper, Hoel predicted that, if hours are reduced, important sectoral shifts will occur between what he called the industry sector and the service sector. These occur because of the different production technologies embodied in the two sectors. (Essentially, he assumed that industry but not services are characterized by the one-man-one-machine technology.) See Hoel, "Employment and Allocation Effects."

Chapter Ten. Two Scenarios

1. Since the emphasis here is on long-term effects, short- or medium-term effects are ignored. Hence, the process by which hours are reduced is not discussed here. It must be admitted, however, that this process could under extreme circumstances have long-term consequences. An abrupt reduction in hours (with consequent declines in real wages per employee, corporate profits, and other indexes of prosperity) by one-quarter could have a number of abrasive social results, with possible long-term effects.
2. Barzel and McDonald, "Assets, Subsistence, and the Supply Curve of Labor."
3. See Owen, *Working Lives,* and Owen, *Working Hours,* as well as the references cited in these publications for econometric evidence of these interpretations of the stability in hours.
4. See Shank, "Preferred Hours of Work."
5. See Owen, *Working Lives,* and Owen, *Working Hours,* for statistical estimations.

6. It is also possible that increased female participation will yield a change in male income-leisure preferences: that the male whose wife is employed is less likely to need income and more likely to want time off to help with housework.

7. White, *Working Hours: Assessing the Potential,* apparently misunderstood my position on this point. To say that higher wages per hour caused earlier hours reduction does not deny that hours reduction also contributed to an increase in hourly wages (due to reduced fatigue, and hence higher productivity and wages). The exogenous factor here is the efficiency wage—the price paid by the employer per unit of effective labor input. As this rises, workers split the melon by asking for more leisure as well as higher income. The result is a further increase in hourly wages as shorter hours permit an increase in the amount of effective labor input supplied per hour. These several factors can be combined in a single model of hours determination. These arguments are discussed in detail in Owen, *Price of Leisure,* and Owen, *Working Hours.* Some empirical tests of the fatigue factor in an integrated demand and supply model of labor is offered in Owen, *Price of Leisure.*

Chapter Eleven. Labor Efficiency

1. Johnston, *Workforce 2000,* p. xix.
2. A familiar theme in the writings of Marxian economists.
3. Johnston, *Workforce 2000.* But see also chapter 12 below for a discussion of the likely negative effect of hours reduction on capital investment.
4. See note 11, chapter 5.
5. One should not endeavor to make an overly specific forecast of effects here, since participation is responsive to a number of factors. For example, a decline in the work ethic accompanied by a reduction in the workweek might be accompanied by a decrease in the number of older people working (the work ethic effect) and by continued increases in female labor force participation (because of the reduction in the workweek). This would be plausible if one reason for working is to have one's own income, regardless of family earnings. The pensioner has personal income independent of his effort, but the housewife must enter the labor market to obtain it. Earlier writers endeavored to speculate on the effects of hours reduction on labor force participation, but no consensus was obtained.
6. Another difference is that unemployment is not assumed to be high in the long-term analysis. As a result, the employer cannot be assumed to have the additional bargaining power that high unemployment provides.
7. Compare the extended discussion in Owen, *Working Hours,* including the lengthier treatment of reasons for low pay to part-time employees. The present discussion is based on this treatment.
8. While part-timers may have about the same turnover rates as full-timers, their shorter weekly schedules mean that they put in many fewer hours in the course of their employment. Hence, fixed per-employee costs have to be spread over perhaps half as many hours, reducing the efficiency with which the part-timer

can be employed. For turnover rates, see Nollen and Martin, "Alternative Work Schedules."

9. See Owen, *Working Hours.*

10. However, it would not be as negative as a reduction in the twenty hours or less averaged by the part-timer.

11. See ibid.

12. But even so, the range of possible forecast error is very large. For example, in either scenario, hours reduction is likely to have serious negative effects on national economic objectives (as discussed in the next two chapters). And we know that Americans have a long-standing tradition of turning to educational reform to solve national problems. It would be in accord with this tradition for a decline in the work ethic in the workplace to give rise to strong demand for reforms in the schools, which would increase the amount of work required from students.

13. This conclusion could be moderated in a variant of the first scenario, in which hours reduction is still in conformance with preferences but occurs in large measure because of a desire to divide market and household work more evenly between the sexes.

Chapter Twelve. National Output

1. But see Hirsch and Addison, *Economic Analysis of Unions,* for a summary of evidence that union demands that reduce industry profitability also reduce investment in that industry.

2. Economies of scale, constraints of energy and materials supplies, and other factors could of course mean that equiproportionate reduction in labor and in capital stock would yield a reduction in output that was more or less in proportion to the reduction in these factor inputs.

3. Marshall, *Principles of Economics.*

4. Compare the more recent discussion in Hoel, "Short- and Long-Run Effects of Reduced Working Time."

5. Useful discussions of the relations between shift work, capital utilization, and capital intensity can be found in Robinson, "Allocation of Time Across the Day"; Betancourt and Clague, "Economic Analysis of Capital Utilization"; Winston, *Timing of Economic Activities;* Winston, "Theory of Capital Utilization and Idleness," and the references cited there; and Mann, "Capital Heterogeneity, Capital Utilization, and the Demand for Shiftworkers." An earlier work, Marris, *Economics of Capital Utilization,* is especially useful on these points.

6. Compare the data in Foss, *Changing Utilization of Fixed Capital.*

7. Compare section D of the appendix.

8. See section C of the appendix.

9. Output,
$$O = .376(WH)[C/n(1 - P)]^{1/4}.$$

C is two; W is assumed to be fifty weeks.

10. If a shift worker is defined as a full-timer who neither begins work between 6:30 and 9:30 in the morning nor ends work between 2:30 and 6:30 in the afternoon, about one in nine workers in the entire nonagricultural economy may be said to be shift workers. For manufacturing, see U.S. Bureau of Labor Statistics, *Area Wage Surveys,* p. 93.
11. Foss, *Changes in the Workweek of Fixed Capital.*
12. Useful discussions of the social and medical costs of shift work are to be found in Maurice, *Shiftwork;* Rentos and Shepard, *Shift Work and Health;* and Tasto and Colligan, "Health Consequences of Shiftwork."
13. Again, this does not imply that hours reduction might not be accompanied by a large increase in shift work: as we have seen, this could occur for a number of reasons not related to hours reduction.
14. More specific depreciation equations can be assumed. Let depreciation be a weighted average of the amount of capital stock and of utilization,

$$D = a[bC + (1 - b)H(1/1 - P)C].$$

Each machine is used $H/1 - P$ hours. If $C/O = mi/O$,

$$i/O = \frac{(I/O)}{1 + ma\,[b + (1 - b)\,(H/1 - P)]},$$

and

$$i/I = \frac{1}{1 + ma\,[b + (1 - b)\,(H/1 - P)]} = v.$$

Here, $E_{v,H}$ is between zero and minus one. The relative effects of depreciation vary directly with the relative importance of D in gross investment (depending on C/O and on the rate of depreciation) and also with the extent to which depreciation is increased by utilization. Only if both are important will $E_{v,H}$ be significantly different from zero.

Chapter Thirteen. Social and Economic Consequences

1. International Labor Organization, "Working Time à la Carte."
2. A slowdown of the substitution of nonhuman for human resources in production will, ceteris paribus, have a negative effect on the rate of growth of output per hour and hence (according to the argument advanced in chapter 12) impact negatively on the prospects for hours reduction. But it is also relevant to the discussion of the effects *on* energy and materials management of hours reduction, should that policy be adopted.
3. Since the effects of hours reduction on the management of materials and energy are somewhat speculative—inasmuch as they depend in part on political and social reactions to future materials, energy, and labor supply restraints— one might consider some alternative scenarios. For example, some advocates of the antigrowth viewpoint urge a return to a simpler life on philosophical

grounds, and use energy shortages as an argument. If this viewpoint comes to be widely held and generates a movement that simultaneously reduces working hours, energy demands, and, of course, material living standards, the cause of energy conservation presumably could be benefited. On the other hand, in the more likely scenario, in which American consumers continue to press for increases in their material living standard despite future material and energy problems, a substantial cut in working hours—with a proportional cut in income—would be more likely to exacerbate pressure for the substitution of materials and energy for labor as a means to bolster labor productivity, with harmful results for the management of these scarce resources.

4. Owen, *Working Hours.*

5. Linder, *Harried Leisure Class.*

6. A Linder-type analysis would suggest that a reduction in workweeks—or rather the consequently lower income and material living standard—would mean that individuals would have to spend less time in maintaining and repairing their consumer goods simply because they had fewer of them. In this analysis, workers would have a twofold increase in their leisure, since they would work fewer hours for pay and would need to spend fewer hours in household production.

7. Putting the point more abstractly, the net effect of leisure or consumption time of an enforced reduction in hours would depend upon the relative possibilities of substituting them for goods in household production and in leisure. If it is relatively easy to substitute time for goods in household production (i.e., if people are reasonably successful at do-it-yourself activities), and relatively difficult to substitute time for goods in leisure activities (the case if individuals are unwilling to accept a change in their life-styles, which would involve spending more time at less expensive recreational pursuits), more of the potential gain in time would go to household production, and less to leisure time. Some calculations of substitution possibilities (based upon past experience) suggest that, here too, these substitution effects may be roughly offsetting, so that the distribution of additional time between leisure and household production time might not be very different from the present distribution.

8. Best, Bosserman, and Stern, "Income-Free Time Trade-Off Preferences of U.S. Workers."

9. See Owen, *Price of Leisure,* for statistical estimates of the influence of leisure on recreation demand, holding income constant.

10. This assessment accords well with the leisure activity analysis developed by Gary Becker. In the application of this theory to recreation (in Owen, ibid.), the demand for leisure activity yields as inputs derived demands for leisure time and recreation spending. The two are substitutes, in that the same amount of leisure activity can be produced by different combinations of leisure time and recreational spending. Hence, recreational spending can expand without an increase in leisure time, if the individual has the necessary income.

Chapter Fourteen. Policy Considerations

1. See the discussion of work incentives in Owen, *School Inequality and the Welfare State.*
2. But see the ambitious program set forth in Reid, "Hours of Work and Overtime Policies." Reid would extend choice over hours of work to employees throughout the province of Ontario.
3. For an analysis of how a simple change in shift arrangements can improve employee attitudes towards evening and night shifts, see Owen, "Changing from a Rotating to a Permanent Shift System in the Detroit Police Department."

BIBLIOGRAPHY AND REFERENCES

Abraham, Katharine G. "Flexible Staffing Arrangements: Model and Some Evidence." Working paper, Brookings, September 1986.

Allen, Richard. "The Economic Effects of a Shorter Working Week." Government Service Working Paper 33; Treasury Working Paper 14, London, June 1980.

"Annual Working Time Will Be Cut by 600 Hours by Year 2000." *Japan Economic Journal,* May 7, 1985, p. 8.

Ashenfelter, Orley. "Compliance with the Minimum Wage Law." *Journal of Political Economy* 87 (1979): 333–50.

Barzel, Y., and R. J. McDonald. "Assets, Subsistence, and the Supply Curve of Labor." *American Economic Review* 87 (1973): 621–33.

Becker, Gary S. "A Theory of the Production and Allocation of Effort." Working Paper 184, National Bureau of Economic Research, Washington, D.C., July 1977.

———. "Human Capital, Effort, and the Sexual Division of Labor." *Journal of Labor Economics* 3 (1985): S33–S89.

Belton, Terrence, Saul H. Hymans, and Cara Lown. "The Dynamics of the Michigan Quarterly Econometric Model of the U.S. Economy." Discussion Paper R-108.81, Department of Economics, University of Michigan, December 1981.

Benjamin, Gerald A. "Shift Workers." *Personnel Journal* 63 (June 1984): 72–76.

Bennett, Roy, and Frank Pressman. "Is It Time for the Four-Day Work Week?" *Social Policy* 15 (Summer 1984): inside cover.

Best, Fred. *Work Sharing. Issues, Policy Options and Prospects.* Kalamazoo: Upjohn, 1981.

Best, Fred, Phillip Bosserman, and Barry Stern. "Income-Free Time Trade-Off Preferences of U.S. Workers: A Review of Literature and Indicators." *Leisure Studies,* in press.

Betancourt, Roger R., and Christopher Clague. "An Econometric Analysis of Capital Utilization." *International Economic Review* 19 (Feb. 1978): 211–27.

Blyton, Paul. *Changes in Working Time. An International Review.* New York: St. Martin's, 1985.

———. "The Working Time Debate in Western Europe." *Industrial Relations* 26 (Spring 1987): 204–7.

Bolle, Michael, Ulrike Fischer, and Burkhard Strumpel. "Research Project: Duration of Working Time and the Possible Employment, Output and Other Consequences of Changing the Present Duration and Pattern. A Summary of the Major Findings." Mimeo., Forschungsstelle Sozialokonomik der Arbeit, Freie Universitat, Berlin, February 1980.

Bonjer, F. H. "Temporal Factors and Physiological Load." In W. T. Singleton, J. G. Fox, and D. Whitfield, *Measurement of Man at Work*. London: Taylor and Francis, 1971.

Booth, Alison, and Fabio Schiantarelli. "Employment Effects of a Shorter Working Week: What Do Union Models Predict?" Mimeo., rev., City University and Essex University, January 1986.

Bowles, Samuel. "The Production Process in a Competitive Economy." *American Economic Review* 75 (1985): 16-36.

Brady, Rosemary. "Short Time." *Forbes,* May 6, 1985, pp. 48, 51.

Bregger, John E. "The Current Population Survey: A Historical Perspective and BLS' Role." *Monthly Labor Review* 107 (June 1984): 8-14.

Brown, David G. "Hours and Output." In C. E. Dankert, F. C. Mann, and A. R. Northrup, *Hours of Work*. New York: Harper and Row, 1965.

Brunstad, Rolf Jens, and Tore Holm. "Can Shorter Hours Solve the Problem of Unemployment?" Paper presented at the European meeting of the Econometric Society, Madrid, September 1984.

Burawoy, Michael. *Manufacturing Consent: Changes in the Labor Process under Monopoly Capitalism*. Chicago: University of Chicago Press, 1979.

Burgoon, Bennett, and Robert D. St. Louis. "The Impact of Work Sharing on Selected Motorola Units." Unpublished working paper, October 1984.

Butler, Richard, and John D. Worrall. "Work Injury Compensation and the Duration of Nonwork Spells." *Economic Journal* 95 (Sept. 1985): 714-24.

Cahill, Marion. *Shorter Hours*. New York: Columbia University Press, 1932.

Calmfors, Lars. "Employment Policies, Wage Formation and Trade Union Behavior in a Small Open Economy." *Scandinavian Journal of Economics* 84 (1982): 345-73.

———. "Work Sharing, Employment, and Wages." *European Economic Review* 27 (Apr. 1985): 293-309.

Calmfors, Lars, and Michael Hoel. "Work Sharing, Overtime and Shiftwork." Seminar Paper 336, Institute of International Economic Studies, University of Stockholm, September 1985.

Casey, Bernard. "Governmental Measures to Promote Part Time Working. Experiences in Belgium, France, Great Britain, The Netherlands, and the Federal Republic of Germany." IIM/LMP 83-26, Wissenschaftszentrum Berlin, November 1983.

———. "Worksharing for Young Persons—Recent Experiences in Great Britain, the Federal Republic of Germany, and the Netherlands." IIM/LMP 84-13a, Wissenschaftszentrum Berlin, August 1984.

———. "Governmental Measures Promoting Part Time Work for Young Persons: Case Studies from Belgium, France, Great Britain, FR Germany, and Sweden." IIM/LMP 84-18, Wissenschaftszentrum Berlin, September 1984.

Chang, Julius C. "An Econometric Model of the Short Run Demand for Workers and Hours in the U.S. Auto Industry." *Journal of Econometrics* 22 (1983): 301-16.

Chan-lee, James H., and Hirimi Kato. "A Comparison of Simulation Properties of National Econometric Models." *OECD Economic Studies,* no. 2 (Spring 1984): 109-50.

Charpin, Jean-Michel. "The Adaptation of Working Time as a Response to the Unemployment Problem." In *Europe's Stagflation,* ed. Michael Emerson. Oxford: Clarendon, 1984.

Cohodas, Nadine. "Public Employers, Unions Join Forces: Fast Congressional Action Solves Worker Overtime Issue." *Congressional Quarterly Report,* November 16, 1985, pp. 2379-80.

Combault, Phillipe. "Le travail à temps partiel en 1984." *Les Collections de l'INSEE,* September 1985, pp. 146-53.

Combault, Phillipe, François Peronnet, and François Rocherieux. "Temps partiel en hausse parmi les femmes salariées." *Collections de l'INSEE,* September 1985, pp. 133-45.

Commission of the European Communities. "Work-Sharing: Meeting of the Standing Committee on Employment." Commission Staff Paper Sec(78) 740, Commission of the European Communities, Brussels, February 20, 1978.

———. "Work-Sharing—Objectives and Effects." Commission Staff Paper Sec(78) 740, Commission of the European Communities, Brussels, February 24, 1978.

———. "Adaptation of Working Time." *European Economy,* no. 5 (1980): 85-119.

———. "Memorandum on the Reduction and Reorganisation of Worktime." Commission Staff Paper Com(82) 809, Commission of the European Communities, Brussels, December 10, 1982.

———. "Draft Council Recommendation on the Reduction and Reorganisation of Working Time." Commission Staff Paper Com (83) 543, Commission of the European Communities, Brussels, September 16, 1983.

Coulaures, Jacques. "Reduction de la durée du travail: La Fin d'un archaisme Malthusian?" *Critiques de l'Economie Politique,* July/September 1984, pp. 67-75.

Craine, Roger. "On the Service Flow from Labor." *Review of Economic Studies* 40 (Jan. 1973): 39-46.

Cristofari, Marie-France, and Jennifer Bue. "Horaires et aménagement du temps de travail des salariés en Mars 1984." *Collections de l'INSEE,* November 1985, pp. 67-74.

Cross, Gary S. "The Quest for Leisure: Reassessing the Eight-Hour Day in France." *Journal of Social History* 18 (Winter 1984): 195-216.

Crowley, R. W., and E. Huth. "An International Comparison of Work Sharing Programs." *Relations industrielles* 38 (1983): 636-47.

Cugno, Franco, and Mario Ferrero. "Individual Incentives by Adjusting Work Hours: Bellamy's Egalitarian Economy." *Journal of Comparative Economics* 8 (1984): 182-206.

Cuvillier, Rolande. *The Reduction of Working Time.* Geneva: International Labor Organization, 1984.

Dagsvik, John K., Olav Ljones, Steinar Storm, and Tom Wennemo. "The Impact on Labor Supply of a Shorter Workday: A Microeconometric Discrete/Continuous Choice Approach." Paper presented at the WZB [Wissenschaftszentrum Berlin] Conference on Employment, Unemployment, and Hours of Work, Berlin, September 17-19, 1986.

Dahl, Shirley J., and Karen L. Hooks. "Women Accountants, Today and Tomorrow." *CPA Journal* 55 (Jan. 1985): 20, 22-25.

Dawkins, Peter. "Non-Standard Hours of Work and Penalty Rates in Australia." *Journal of Industrial Relations* 27 (Sept. 1985): 329-49.

de Meza, David. "The Fourth Commandment: Is It Pareto Efficient?" *Economic Journal* 94 (June 1984): 379-83.

De Regt, Erik R. "Shorter Working Time in a Model of a Firm. Theory and Estimation." Working Paper, Institute for Economic Research, Erasmus University, Rotterdam, 1984.

———. "Labor Demand and Standard Working Time in Dutch Manufacturing 1954-1982." Paper presented at the WZB [Wissenschaftszentrum Berlin] Conference on Employment, Unemployment, and Hours of Work, Berlin, September 17-19, 1986.

Deutschmann, Christoph. "A Cultural View of Japanese Working Hours." Speech delivered at Tohuku University International House, October 1985.

———. "Working Hours in West Germany and Japan." In *Structural Conditions of Industrial Relations in West Germany and Japan,* ed. J. Bergmann and S. Tokanaga. forthcoming.

Doeringer, Peter, and Michael Piore. *Internal Labor Markets and Manpower Analysis.* Lexington, Mass.: Heath, 1971.

Donaldsen, David, and B. Curtis Eaton. "Person-Specific Costs of Production: Hours of Work, Rates of Pay, Labour Contracts." *Canadian Journal of Economics* 17 (Aug. 1984): 441-49.

Drèze, Jacques H. "Work Sharing: Why? How? How Not. . . ." *Economic Papers* 42, Commission of the European Communities, December 1985.

Drèze, Jacques H., and Franco Modigliani. "The Trade-Off Between Real Wages and Employment in an Open Economy (Belgium)." *European Economic Review* 15 (1981): 1-40.

du Bois, Paul. "Vingt ans après: Les Projections 1985 confrontées à la réalité." *Economie et Statistique* 177 (May 1985): 3-10.

Edwards, Richard. *Contested Terrain: The Transformation of the Workplace in the Twentieth Century.* New York: Basic Books, 1979.

Ehrenberg, Ronald G. *Fringe Benefits and Overtime Behavior.* Lexington, Mass.: Heath, 1971.

Ehrenberg, Ronald G., Pamela Rosenberg, and Jeanne Li. "Part Time Employment in the United States." Paper presented at the WZB [Wissenschaftszentrum Berlin] Conference on Employment, Unemployment, and Hours of Work, Berlin, September 17-19, 1986.

Ehrenberg, Ronald G., and Paul L. Schumann. *Longer Hours or More Jobs?* Ithaca: New York State School of Industrial and Labor Relations, Cornell University, 1982.

Emerson, Michael, ed. *Europe's Stagflation.* Oxford: Clarendon, 1984.

Employment Gazette (Great Britain). Various issues.

English, Carey W. "Now It's Bosses Who Are Giving Orders Again." *U.S. News and World Report,* February 11, 1985.

———. "Behind Hiring of More Temporary Employees." *U.S. News and World Report,* February 25, 1985.

Fair, Ray C. "Excess Labor and the Business Cycle." *American Economic Review* 75 (1985): 239-45.

Fay, Jon A., and James L. Medoff. "Labor and Output over the Business Cycle: Some Direct Evidence." *American Economic Review* 75 (1985): 638-55.

Feldstein, Martin S. "Specification of the Labour Input in the Aggregate Production Function." *Review of Economic Studies* 34 (1967): 375-86.

Filer, Randall K. "People and Productivity: Effort Supply Viewed by Economists and Psychologists." In *Handbook of Behavioral Economics,* ed. B. Gilad and S. Kaish. Greenwich, Conn.: JAI Press, 1986.

Fitzroy, Felix R. "Work-Sharing and Insurance Policy: A Cure for Stagflation." *Kyklos* 34 (1981): 432-47.

————. "Employment and Hours in Equilibrium and Disequilibrium." Paper presented at the WZB [Wissenschaftszentrum Berlin] Conference on Employment, Unemployment, and Hours of Work, Berlin, September 17-19, 1986.

Fitzroy, Felix R., and Robert A. Hart. "Hours of Work, Layoffs and Unemployment Insurance: Theory and Practice in the U.S. and Elsewhere," IIM/IP 82-44, Wissenschaftszentrum Berlin, December 1982.

————. "Hours, Layoffs and Unemployment Insurance Funding: Theory and Practice in an International Perspective." *Economic Journal* 95 (Sept. 1985): 700-713.

Ford, Henry. "Why I Favor Five Days Work with Six Days Pay." *The World's Work* 52 (Oct. 1926): 613-16.

Foss, Murray F. *Changes in the Workweek of Fixed Capital: U.S. Manufacturing 1929 to 1976.* Washington, D.C.: American Enterprise Institute, 1981.

————. *Changing Utilization of Fixed Capital: An Element in Long-Term Growth.* Washington, D.C.: American Enterprise Institute, 1984.

Franz, Wolfgang. "Is Less More? The Current Discussion about Reduced Working Time in Western Germany: A Survey of the Debate." *Zeitschrift fur die gesamte Staatswissenschaft* 140 (1984): 626-54.

Frayssinet, Daniel. "La Durée annuelle du travail en 1981 et 1982—premiers résultats." *Collections de l'INSEE,* September 1985, pp. 5-14.

Freiman, Marc, and William D. Marder. "Changes in the Hours Worked by Physicians, 1970-1980." *American Journal of Public Health* 74 (Dec. 1984): 1348-52.

Furstenberg, Friedrich. "The Regulation of Working Time in the Federal Republic of Germany." *Labour and Society* 10 (May 1985): 144-50.

Gannon, Martin J., Douglas L. Norland, and Franklin E. Robeson. "Shift Work Has Complex Effects on Lifestyles and Work Habits." *Personnel Administrator* 11 (May 1983): 93-97.

Gans, Herbert J. "Toward the 32-Hour Workweek." *Social Policy* 15 (Winter 1985): 58-61.

Gohmann, Stephan F., and Robert L. Clark. "Social Security Benefit Acceptance and the Retirement Decision." Faculty Working Paper 53, Department of Economics and Business, North Carolina State University, July 1984.

Grais, Bernard. *Layoffs and Short-time Working.* Paris: OECD, 1983.

Grossin, William. "Temps de travail et temps libre." *Revue Français des affaires sociales,* no. 2 (1984): 9-20.

Gunton, George. *Principles of Social Progress.* New York: Putnam and Sons, 1892.

———. *Wealth and Progress.* New York: Appleton, 1897.

Gutchess, Jocelyn F. *Employment Security in Action: Strategies That Work.* New York: Pergamon, 1985.

Haber, Phillip J., and Donald J. Petersen. "Arbitration and the Shortened Work Week: No Easy Answer." *Personnel* 62 (Mar. 1985): 8-10.

Hamel, Harvey R. "New Data Series on Involuntary Part-Time Work." *Monthly Labor Review* 108 (Mar. 1985): 42-43.

Hamermesh, Daniel S. "The Demand for Workers and the Effects of Job Security Policies: Theory and Evidence." Paper presented at the WZB [Wissenschaftszentrum Berlin] Conference on Employment, Unemployment, and Hours of Work, Berlin, September 17-19, 1986.

Harrison, Alan. "A Labour-Market Model of Unemployment Insurance." IIM/LMP 82-19, Wissenschaftszentrum Berlin, August 1982.

Hart, R. A. "Unemployment Insurance and the Firm's Employment Strategy: A European and United States Comparison." *Kyklos* 35 (1982): 648-72.

———. "The Phillips Curve and Cyclical Manhour Variation." *Oxford Economic Papers* 35 (1983): 186-201.

———. *Shorter Working Time. A Dilemma for Collective Bargaining.* Paris: OECD, 1984.

———. "Work Sharing and Factor Prices." *European Economic Review* 24 (1984): 165-88.

———. "The Employment and Hours Effect of a Marginal Employment Subsidy: A Microeconomic Approach." Mimeo., Department of Economics, University of Stirling, May 1986.

———. *Working Time and Employment.* London: Allen and Unwin, 1987.

Hart, R. A., and Peter Macgregor. "The Returns to Labour Services in West German Manufacturing Industry." IIM/LMP 83-14, Wissenschaftszentrum Berlin, June 1983.

Hart, R. A., and Seiichi Kawasaki. "Payroll Taxes and Factor Demand." IIM/LMP 85-1, Wissenschaftszentrum Berlin, January 1985.

Hart, R. A., and Nicholas Wilson. "The Demand for Workers and Hours: Micro Evidence from the U.K. Metal Working Industry." Paper presented at the WZB [Wissenschaftszentrum Berlin] Conference on Employment, Unemployment, and Hours of Work, September 17-19, 1986.

Hashimoto, Masanori, and John Raisian. "Employment, Hours of Work, and Wage Adjustments in Japan and the United States." Mimeo., Indiana University and Hoover Institute, August 1986.

Hedges, Janice Neipert. "Absence from Work—Measuring the Hours Lost." *Monthly Labor Review* 100 (Oct. 1977): 16-23.

———. Discussant, "Work Sharing: New Experiences." In *Proceedings of the Thirty-Eighth Annual Meeting of the Industrial Relations Research Association.* New York: IRRA, 1986.

Hedges, Janice Neipert, and Edward S. Sekscenski. "Workers on Late Shifts in a Changing Economy." *Monthly Labor Review* 102 (Sept. 1979): 14-22.

Hedges, Janice Neipert, and Daniel E. Taylor. "Recent Trends in Worktime: Hours Edge Downward." *Monthly Labor Review* 103 (Mar. 1980): 3-11.

Henize, John. "An Evaluation of the Effects of a Reduction in Working Hours Using the German Employment Policy Model." Mimeo., Gesellschaft für Mathematik und Datenverarbeitung, West Germany, August 1980.

———. "Can a Shorter Workweek Reduce Unemployment? A German Simulation Study." *Simulation* 37 (Nov. 1981): 145-56.

Henle, Peter. "Recent Growth of Paid Leisure for U.S. Workers." *Monthly Labor Review* 84 (Mar. 1962): 249-57.

Henning, Dale. "Paid Vacations under Collective Bargaining Agreements, 1949." *Monthly Labor Review* 69 (Nov. 1949): 518-22.

Hicks, Sir John R. *Theory of Wages.* New York: Macmillan, 1932. Reprint, New York: Peter Smith, 1948.

Hirsch, Barry T., and John T. Addison. *The Economic Analysis of Unions.* Boston: Allen and Unwin, 1986.

Hoel, Michael. "Short- and Long-Run Effects of Reduced Working Time in a Unionized Economy." Memorandum 10, Department of Economics, University of Oslo, February 6, 1984.

———. "Can Shorter Working Time Reduce Unemployment?" Memorandum 28, Department of Economics, University of Oslo, November 15, 1985.

———. "Employment and Allocation Effects of Reducing the Length of Workday." *Economica* 53 (Feb. 1986): 75-85.

Hoel, Michael, and Bent Vale. "Effects of Reduced Working Time in an Economy Where Firms Set Wages." Memorandum 2, Department of Economics, University of Oslo, January 18, 1985.

Houseman, Susan N. "Shorter Working Time and Job Security: Labor Adjustment in the European Steel Industry." Paper presented at the WZB [Wissenschaftszentrum Berlin] Conference on Employment, Unemployment, and Hours of Work, Berlin, September 17-19, 1986.

Hubek, Phillip J., and Donald J. Petersen. "Arbitration and the Shortened Work Week: No Easy Answer." *Personnel* 62 (Mar. 1985): 8-10.

Huber, Gerhard. "Employment Policy and Labor Market Policy: A Linear Model." Paper presented at the WZB [Wissenschaftszentrum Berlin] Conference on Employment, Unemployment, and Hours of Work, Berlin, September 17-19, 1986.

Hunnicutt, Benjamin K. "The End of Shorter Hours." *Labor History* 25 (Summer 1984): 373-404.

IDS/PA European Report 289, May 5, 1987.

INSEE. *Les Collections de l'INSEE. Enquête sur l'emploi, 1984, 1985.* Paris, 1985, 1986.

———. "La Durée annuelle du travail 1970-1983." Mimeo., Institut de la Statistique et des Etudes Economiques, Paris, January 23, 1985.

International Labor Organization. "Working Time à la Carte." *Information* 22 (Dec. 1986): 1.

Ishizuka, Masahiko. "Japan at Random: Flourishing Part-Time Business." *Japan,* April 9, 1985, p. 6.

Jallade, Jean Pierre. *L'Europe à temps partiel.* Paris: Economica, 1982.

———. "Reduction and Adjustment of Working Time: Lessons of the French Experience." *Labour and Society* 10 (May 1985): 151–62.

Janssen, Hans. "Reductions in Working Time, Practical Problems and the Employment Effect in the Federal Republic of Germany: The Example of the Metal-Working Industry." Paper presented at Symposium on Trends in Working Time in Western European Countries: Reductions in Working Time, Geneva, February 11–13, 1986.

Johnston, William B. *Workforce 2000: Work and Workers for the 21st Century.* Indianapolis: Hudson Institute, 1987.

Jones, Stephen G. "The Worksharing Debate in Western Europe." *National Westminister Bank Quarterly Review,* February 1985, pp. 30–41.

Jovanis, Paul P. "Telecommunications and Alternative Work Schedules—Options for Managing Transit Travel Demand." *Urban Affairs Quarterly* 19 (Dec. 1983): 167–89.

Juster, F. Thomas, and Frank P. Stafford, eds. *Time, Goods, and Well-Being.* Ann Arbor: University of Michigan, Institute for Social Research, 1985.

Kato, Takao. "Work-Sharing, Layoffs, and Intrafirm Labour Transfers." Discussion Paper 565, Department of Economics, Queen's University, Kingston, 1984.

Katz, Arnold. "Employment of Students, October 1959." *Monthly Labor Review* 83 (June 1960): 705–10.

Kerachsky, Stuart, Walter Nicholson, Edward Cavin, and Alan Hershey. "An Evaluation of Short-time Compensation Programs." In *Proceedings of the Thirty-Eighth Annual Meeting of the Industrial Relations Research Association.* New York: IRRA, 1986.

Klein, Bruce W. "Missed Work and Lost Hours, May 1985." *Monthly Labor Review* 109 (Nov. 1986): 26–30.

Kunze, Kent. "A New BLS Survey Measures the Ratio of Hours Worked to Hours Paid." *Monthly Labor Review* 107 (June 1984): 3–7.

———. "Hours at Work Increase Relative to Hours Paid." *Monthly Labor Review* 108 (June 1985): 44–46.

Lammers, John C. "Managing Unemployment: The Role of Union Business Agents and the Use of Work Sharing." *Social Policy* 32 (Dec. 1984): 133–43.

Lang, Graeme. "Regional Variations in Worksharing: The Case of Newfoundland." *Canadian Public Policy* 11 (1985): 54–63.

Layard, P. R. G., and S. J. Nickell. "The Case for Subsidizing Extra Jobs." *Economic Journal* 90 (Mar. 1980): 51–73.

Lazear, Edward P. "Agency, Earnings Profiles, Productivity and Hours Restrictions." *American Economic Review* 71 (Sept. 1981): 606–20.

———. "Employment-at-Will, Job Security, and Work Incentives." Mimeo., University of Chicago and Hoover Institute, June 1986.

Lea, Stephen E. G., Roger M. Tarpy, and Paul Webley. *The Individual and the Economy: A Survey of Economic Psychology.* New York: Cambridge University Press, 1987.

Leslie, Derek, and John Wise. "The Productivity of Hours in U.K. Manufacturing and Production Industries." *Review of Economic Studies* 90 (Mar. 1980): 74–84.

Leveson, Irving F. "Reduction in Hours of Work as a Source of Productivity Growth." *Journal of Political Economy* 72 (Apr. 1967): 199–204.

Lewis, H. G. "Hours of Work and Hours of Leisure." Paper presented at the Ninth Annual Meeting of the Industrial Relations Research Association, Cleveland, 1957.

Lilien, David M. "The Cyclical Pattern of Temporary Layoffs in United States Manufacturing." *Review of Economics and Statistics* 6 (Feb. 1980): 24–31.

Lindbeck, Assar, and Dennis Snower. "Involuntary Unemployment as an Insider-Outsider Dilemma." Seminar Paper 282, Institute for International Economic Studies, University of Stockholm, July 1984.

Linder, Staffen. *The Harried Leisure Class*. New York: Columbia University Press, 1970.

Loos, Jocelyn. "Le Syndicalism à l'épreuve des expériences d'aménagement du temps de travail." *Revue Français des affaires sociales*, no. 2 (1984): 21–38.

Macarow, David. "Overcoming Unemployment. Some Radical Proposals." *Futurist* 19 (Apr. 1985): 19–24.

McCarthy, Maureen E., and Gail S. Rosenberg. *Worksharing: Case Studies*. Kalamazoo: Upjohn, 1981.

McDonald, Richard J. "The 'Underground Economy' and BLS Statistical Data." *Monthly Labor Review* 109 (Jan. 1984): 4–18.

MacFadyen, Heather Wood. "Motivational Constructs in Psychology." In *Economic Psychology: Interaction in Theory and Application*, ed. Alan J. MacFadyen and Heather Wood MacFadyen. Amsterdam: Elsevier Science Publishers, North-Holland, 1986.

McKee, Michael, and Edwin G. West. "Minimum Wage Effects on Part-Time Employment." *Economic Inquiry* 22 (July 1984): 421–28.

MaCoy, Ramelle, and Martin J. Moran. *Short-time Compensation. A Formula for Work Sharing*. New York: Pergamon, 1984.

Magnier, Gérard. "Les Enterprises signataires de solidarité préretraite. Bilan statistiques sur la période 1982–1983." Paris, *Collections de l'INSEE*, September 1984, pp. 15–26.

Malcomson, James M. "Unemployment and the Efficiency Wage Hypothesis." *Economic Journal* 91 (Dec. 1981): 848–66.

Mann, Barbara S. "Capital Heterogeneity, Capital Utilization, and the Demand for Shiftworkers." *Canadian Journal of Economics* 17 (Aug. 1984): 450–70.

Marchand, Olivier, Daniel Rault, and Etienne Turpin. "Des 40 heures aux 39 heures: Processus et réactions des entreprises." *Economie et statistique*, April 1983, pp. 3–15.

Marris, Robin. *The Economics of Capital Utilization: A Report on Multiple-Shift Work*. Cambridge: Cambridge University Press, 1964.

Marsden, David. *Working Time Statistics, Methods and Measurement in the European Community: A Report to Eurostat*. Luxemburg: Office of Official Publications of the European Community, 1984.

Marshall, Alfred. *Principles of Economics*. London: Macmillan, 1920.

Maurice, Marc. *Shiftwork*. Geneva: International Labor Organization, 1975.

Melbin, Murray. "Night as Frontier." *American Sociological Review* 43 (Feb. 1978): 3-22.

Meltz, Noah M. Discussant, "Work Sharing: New Experiences." In *Proceedings of the Thirty-Eighth Annual Meeting of the Industrial Relations Research Association*. New York: IRRA, 1986.

Metcalf, David, Stephen Nickell, and Ray Richardson. "The Structure of Hours and Earnings in British Manufacturing Industry." Working Paper, rev., London School of Economics, February 1974.

Miller, Roger LeRoy. "The Reserve Labour Hypothesis: Some Tests of Its Implications." *Economic Journal* 81 (March 1971): 17-35.

Mincer, Jacob. "Inter-Country Comparisons of Labor Force Trends and of Related Developments: An Overview." Working Paper 1438, National Bureau of Economic Research, August 1984.

Morand, Martin J. Discussant, "Work Sharing: New Experiences." In *Proceedings of the Thirty-Eighth Annual Meeting of the Industrial Relations Research Association*. New York: IRRA, 1986.

Moss, Richard Loring, and Thomas D. Curtis. "The Economics of Flextime." *Journal of Behavioral Economics* 14 (Summer 1985): 95-114.

Moy, Joyanna, and Constance Sorrentino. "Unemployment, Labor Force Trends, and Layoff Practices in 10 Countries." *Monthly Labor Review* 104 (Dec. 1981): 3-13.

Murrell, K. F. H. "Temporal Factors in Light Work." In W. T. Singleton, J. G. Fox, and D. Whitfield, *Measurement of Man at Work*. London: Taylor and Francis, 1971.

Nemirow, Martin. "Work-Sharing Approaches: Past and Present." *Monthly Labor Review* 107 (Sept. 1984): 34-39.

Netherlands Council of Employment Federations. "Towards Individualization of Working Time." Discussion paper, Working Time, The Hague, December 1980.

Netherlands Council of Employment Federations. "A Close Look at Working Time." Discussion paper, Working Time, The Hague, March 1983.

Newman, Barry. "European Debate: Can Shorter Workweek Bring More Jobs?" *Wall Street Journal*, May 14, 1984.

Nollen, Stanley D., and Virginia H. Martin. "Alternative Work Schedules, Part 2: Permanent Part-Time Employment." New York: AMACOM, 1978.

Northrup, Herbert, and Herbert R. Brinberg. *Economics of the Workweek*. Studies in Business 24. New York: National Industrial Conference Board, 1950.

O'Connor, Charles M. "Late-Shift Employment in Manufacturing Industries." *Monthly Labor Review* 93 (Nov. 1970): 37-42.

Odagari, Hiroyuki. "Firm Employment Policy and Macroeconomic Stability: Theory and International Comparison." Discussion Paper 292, Institute of Socio-Economic Planning, University of Tsukuba, January 1986.

OECD. *Labor Market Flexibility*. Paris: OECD, 1986.

OECD Secretariat. "The Current Debate on Working Time Adjustments in OECD Member Countries." Mimeo. Directorate for Social Affairs, Manpower and Education, OECD, December 16, 1983.

Oswald, Andrew J. "The Economic Theory of Trade Unions: An Introductory Survey." *Scandinavian Journal of Economics* 87 (1985): 160-96.

Oudiz, Gilles, Emmanuel Raoul, and Henri Sterdyniak. "Reduire la durée du travail. Quelles conséquences?" *Economie et statistique,* May 1979, pp. 3-17.

Owen, John D. *The Price of Leisure.* Rotterdam: Rotterdam University Press, 1969; Montreal: McGill-Queens University Press, 1970.

———. *School Inequality and the Welfare State.* Baltimore: Johns Hopkins University Press, 1975.

———. *Working Hours.* Lexington, Mass.: Heath, 1979.

———. "Changing from a Rotating to a Permanent Shift System in the Detroit Police Department: Effects on Employee Attitudes and Behavior." *Labor Law Journal,* August 1985.

———. *Working Lives.* Lexington, Mass.: Heath, 1986.

Pencavel, John. "Wages and Employment under Trade Unionism: Microeconomic Models and Macroeconomic Applications." *Scandinavian Journal of Economics* 87 (1985): 197-225.

Pigou, A. C. *Economics of Welfare.* London: Macmillan, 1932.

Pohlimerier, Winfried, and Heinz Konig. "A Dynamic Model of Labor Utilization." Paper presented at the WZB [Wissenschaftszentrum Berlin] Conference on Employment, Unemployment, and Hours of Work, September 17-19, 1986.

Pollak, Robert A., and Michael Wachter. "The Relevance of the Household Production Function and Its Implications for the Allocation of Time." *Journal of Political Economy* 83 (1975): 255-77.

Poper, Franklin J. "A Critical Evaluation of the Empirical Evidence Underlying the Relationship Between Hours of Work and Labor Productivity." Ph.D. dissertation, New York University, 1970.

Presser, Harriett B. "Job Characteristics of Spouses and Their Work Shifts." *Demography* 21 (Nov. 1984): 575-89.

Ralston, David A., William P. Anthony, and David J. Gustafson. "Employees May Love Flextime, but What Does It Do to the Organization's Productivity?" *Journal of Applied Psychology* 70 (1985): 272-79.

Ramandraivonona, Dera. "La Durée annuelle du travail des salariés en 1981 et 1982. Les Effets de l'ordonnance du 16 Janvier 1982 sur la réduction du temps de travail." *Collections de l'INSEE,* September 1985, pp. 5-70.

"Recent Changes in Hours and Holiday Entitlements—Manual Employees." *Employment Gazette,* March 1987, pp. 131-33.

Reid, Frank. "Hours of Work and Overtime Policies to Reduce Unemployment." A Report to the Ontario Task Force on Hours of Work and Overtime, University of Toronto, September 1986.

Rentos, P. G., and R. D. Shepard, eds. *Shift Work and Health.* Washington, D.C.: U.S. Department of Health, Education, and Welfare, 1976.

Reyher, Lutz. "Draft Report on Hours Worked." Paper submitted to OECD Working Party on Employment and Unemployment Statistics, Paris, 1982.

Robinson, Christopher M. G. F. "Allocation of Time Across the Day: An Analysis of the Demand and Supply of Shiftworkers." Ph.D. dissertation, University of Chicago, 1977.

————. "An Analysis of the Demand and Supply of Shiftworkers." Mimeo., rev., Department of Economics, University of Western Ontario, December 1979.

Robinson, Olive. "The Changing Labour Market: The Phenomenon of Part-Time Employment in Britain." *National Westminister Bank Quarterly Review,* November 1985, pp. 19-29.

Rose, Michael. "Shiftwork: How Does It Affect You?" *American Journal of Nursing* 86 (Apr. 1984): 442-47.

Rosen, Sherwin. "The Supply of Work Schedules and Employment." In *Worktime and Employment.* Washington, D.C.: U.S. Department of Labor, 1978.

Rosenfeld, Carl. "Employment of Students, October 1960." *Monthly Labor Review* 84 (July 1961): 706-14.

Rubinstein, Irving, and Rose Theodore. "Holiday Provisions in Union Agreements, 1950." *Monthly Labor Review* 71 (Jan. 1951): 24-27.

Samuel, Nicole. *Le Temps libre: Un Temps social.* Paris: Librairie des Meridiens, 1984.

Santamaki, Tuire. "The Overtime Pay Premium, Hours of Work, and Employment." Working Paper F-75, Helsinki School of Economics, November 1983.

————. "Employment and Hours Decisions, and the Willingness to Work Overtime Hours." Working Paper F-86, Helsinki School of Economics, March 1984.

————. "Implications of the Non-Homogeneity of Standard and Overtime Hours on the Structure and Cyclical Adjustment of Labor Input." Mimeo., Labor Institute for Economic Research, Finland, 1986.

Santamaki-Vuori, Tuire. "Cyclical Adjustment of Hours and Employment, An Optimal Control Approach to the Behaviour of the Firm." Series A:46, Helsinki School of Economics, January 1986.

Scarth, William M., and Anthony Myatt. "The Real Wage-Employment Relationship." *Economic Journal* 90 (Mar. 1980): 85-94.

Schiff, Frank W. "Issues in Assessing Worksharing." In *Proceedings of the Thirty-Eighth Annual Meeting of the Industrial Relations Research Association.* New York: IRRA, 1986.

Sekscenski, Edward S. *Job Tenure Declines as Work Force Changes.* Special Labor Force Report 235. Washington, D.C.: Government Printing Office, 1979.

Shank, Susan E. "Preferred Hours of Work and Corresponding Earnings." *Monthly Labor Review* 109 (Nov. 1986): 40-44.

Shapiro, C., and J. E. Stiglitz. "Equilibrium Unemployment as a Worker Discipline Device." *American Economic Review* 73 (1984): 433-44.

"Shorter Hours Through National Agreements." *Employment Gazette* (Great Britain) 91 (Oct. 1983): 432-36.

Singleton, W. T., J. G. Fox, and D. Whitfield. *Measurement of Man at Work.* London: Taylor and Francis, 1971.

Snook, Stover H., and Charles H. Irvine. "Psychophysical Studies of Physiological Fatigue Criteria." *Human Factors* 11 (1969): 291-300.

Stafford, Frank P., and Malcolm S. Cohen. "A Model of Work Effort and Productive Consumption." *Journal of Economic Theory* (1974): 333-47.

Stafford, Frank P., and Greg J. Duncan. "The Use of Time and Technology by Households in the United States." In *Time, Goods and Well-Being,* ed. Thomas F. Juster and Frank P. Stafford. Ann Arbor: University of Michigan, Institute for Social Research, 1985.

Statistiches Bundesamt. Institut fur Arbeit und Berufsforschung. Various issues.

Stinson, John F., Jr. "Moonlighting by Women Jumped to Record Highs." *Monthly Labor Review* 109 (Nov. 1986): 22–25.

———. "Moonlighting: A Key to Differences in Measuring Employment Growth." *Monthly Labor Review* 110 (Feb. 1987): 30–31.

Swank, Constance. *Phased Retirement: The European Experience.* Washington, D.C.: National Council for Alternative Work Patterns, 1982.

Taddei, Dominique. "Pour une nouvelle organisation de la production: Allongement de la durée d'utilisation des equipements, aménagements et reduction du temps de travail." Unpublished government report, Paris, September 19, 1985.

Taher, Gabriel. *La Réduction de la durée du travail.* Paris: Edition de la Couverte, 1985.

Tasto, Donald L., and Micael J. Colligan. "Health Consequences of Shiftwork." Report of Stanford Research Institute for the National Institute for Occupational Safety and Health, March 1978.

Topel, Robert, and Finis Welch. "Unemployment Insurance: Survey and Extensions." *Economica* 47 (Aug. 1980): 351–79.

Topel, Robert, Finis Welch, and Laurence Weiss. "Sectoral Uncertainty and Unemployment." Working Paper 384, rev., UCLA Department of Economics, September 1985.

Ure, Andrew. *Philosophy of Manufactures.* London: Charles Knight, 1835.

U.S. Department of Labor, Bureau of Labor Statistics. *Area Wage Surveys: Metropolitan Areas, United States and Regional Summaries, 1975.* Washington, D.C.: Government Printing Office, 1977.

———. *Current Population Survey.* Washington, D.C.: Government Printing Office, various years.

———. *Employee Benefits in Medium and Large Firms, 1984.* Bulletin 2237. Washington, D.C.: Government Printing Office, July 1985.

———. *Employee Benefits in Medium and Large Firms, 1985.* Bulletin 2262. Washington, D.C.: Government Printing Office, July 1986.

———. *Employment and Earnings.* Washington, D.C.: Government Printing Office, various issues.

———. *Handbook of Labor Statistics.* Bulletin 2175. Washington, D.C.: Government Printing Office, December 1983.

———. *Handbook of Labor Statistics.* Bulletin 2217. Washington, D.C.: Government Printing Office, June 1985.

———. *Special Reports on the Labor Force.* Washington, D.C.: Government Printing Office, various issues.

U.S. General Accounting Office. "Reduction in Force Can Sometimes Be More Costly to Agencies then Attrition and Furlough." GAO/PEMD-85-6, July 24, 1985.

van Ginneken, Winter. "Employment and the Reduction of the Workweek: A

Comparison of Seven European Macro-economic Models." *International Labor Review* 123 (Jan./Feb. 1984): 35–52.

Weber, Axel. "Federal Republic of Germany." In *Symposium on Trends in Working Time in Western European Countries: Reductions in Working Time.* Geneva: International Institute for Labour Studies, 1986.

White, Michael. *Working Hours: Assessing the Potential for Reduction.* Geneva: International Labor Office, 1987.

Whitley, J. D., and R. A. Wilson. "The Macroeconomic Merits of a Marginal Employment Subsidy." *Economic Journal* 93 (Dec. 1983): 862–80.

———. "The Impact on Employment of Reduction in the Length of the Working Week." *Cambridge Journal of Economics* 10 (1986): 43–59.

———. "Hours Reduction within Large-Scale Macroeconomic Models: Conflict Between Theory and Practice." Paper presented at the WZB [Wissenschaftszentrum Berlin] Conference on Employment, Unemployment, and Hours of Work, Berlin, September 17–19, 1986.

Williams, Bruce. "Shorter Hours—Increased Employment?" *Three Banks Review.* September 1984, pp. 3–16.

Winston, Gordon C. "The Theory of Capital Utilization and Idleness." *Journal of Economic Literature,* December 1974.

———. *The Timing of Economic Activities.* Cambridge: Cambridge University Press, 1982.

Wise, Leslie. "The Productivity of Hours in U.K. Manufacturing and Production Industries." *Economic Journal* 90 (Mar. 1980): 74–84.

"Working Time in Europe: Two Recent Cases." *Labour and Society* 10 (May 1985): 131–62.

Young, Anne McDougall. "Fewer Students in Workforce as School Age Population Declines." *Monthly Labor Review* 107 (July 1984): 34–37.

Zalusky, John. "Labor's Interest and Concerns with Short Time Compensation." In *Proceedings of the Thirty-Eighth Annual Meeting of the Industrial Relations Research Association.* New York: IRRA, 1986.

INDEX

ABOUT THE AUTHOR

John D. Owen is professor of economics at Wayne State University. He is the author of *Working Lives: The American Workforce since 1920.*

REDUCED WORKING HOURS

Designed by Laury Egan

Composed by Action Comp Co., Inc.,
in Times Roman

Printed by BookCrafters
on 50-lb. Booktext Natural
and bound in Holliston Roxite A